Maldon Salt

Winter Sun

Over-watered
Basil

Parmigiano

Gastro Pub
Green

Rosé

Wait Rose

Lost Khaki

Deaf & Incontinent
Labrador

Roast Chicken

Cornish Weather

FI COTTER CRAIG It would be absolutely true to say that Fi Cotter Craig is a television producer who lives in both London and Norfolk surrounded by Spaniels. However, what is slightly more questionable is whether, having previously only ever written thank-you letters, she is in any way qualified to have co-written this ~~important sociological work~~ impulse-buy loo book.

ZEBEDEE HELM was born into the middle classes one Saturday in November. He has since worked as an artist, was Morris dancing correspondent for the *Lady* and has contributed to *Private Eye*. He has also enjoyed ~~immoderate~~ . . . ~~moderate~~ . . . very little success as a writer and illustrator of children's books.

THE MIDDLE CLASS ABC

Written by Zebedee Helm and Fi Cotter Craig

Illustrations by Zebedee Helm

JOHN MURRAY

First published in Great Britain in 2012 by John Murray (Publishers)
An Hachette UK Company

I

Text © Fi Cotter Craig and Zebedee Helm 2012
Illustrations © Zebedee Helm 2012

The right of Fi Cotter Craig and Zebedee Helm to be identified as
the Authors of the Work has been asserted by them in accordance with
the Copyright, Designs and Patents Act 1988.

A CIP catalogue record for this title is available from the British Library

ISBN 978-1-84854-6806
Ebook ISBN 978-1-84854-6820

Typeset in Mrs Eaves and Gill Sans

Printed by
C&C Printing Offset Co., Ltd., China

John Murray policy is to use papers that are natural, renewable and
recyclable products and made from wood grown in sustainable forests.
The logging and manufacturing processes are expected to conform to
the environmental regulations of the country of origin.

John Murray (Publishers)
338 Euston Road
London NW1 3BH

www.johnmurray.co.uk

To Catherine and Zelda ~~once again~~

is for Allergies...

Now, *please* remember, NO wheat for Rococo

Zoffany has a *massive* dairy *intolerance*. Milk will kill her

Absolutely NO JELLY for Michaelangelo, he has a *hyper* allergy

Zanzibar will die in agony if she so much as *looks* at a nut

Anchovies . . . Small salty fish, found in cans or jars. The cans are quite easy to operate, but once open are a nuisance in the fridge. As for the jars, due to over-wedging, it is almost impossible to remove the fish. Recent reports suggest that there are more anchovies in Middle Class kitchen cupboards (or larders, preferably) than there are swimming in the sea. Like Marmite, you either love them or hate them — we're not sure ourselves.

Can

Can't

Au Pairs . . . It is questionable whether an Au Pair is of any actual use to the household, but they are a Middle Class trophy nevertheless. They can't drive on the left, have no sense of ironing, flirt with husbands, are hopeless with children and eat like horses. Like Cinderella, they dream of marrying a prince, otherwise known as a Premiership footballer.

Army . . . There are few more rousing sights than a regiment of soldiers marching in a straight line and saluting the Queen while wearing very tight trousers with stripes down the side. When they wear camouflage you can't see them at all. Middle Class soldiers are issued with highly desirable double-barrelled job titles like Brigadier-General, Lieutenant-Colonel, Captain-Major and Lieutenant-Lieutenant. All other soldiers are called Privates, which isn't so appealing.

Alcohol . . . Drinking Alcohol is one of the most popular Middle Class hobbies. Keen to pass on the pleasure of a lifetime, Middling parents start watering down wine for their offspring when they're about twelve or thirteen, blissfully unaware that Archimedes and Chaffinch have been at the alcopops and dinner party dregs since they were six.

Alcoholics Anonymous . . . After the watered-down wine it's only a matter of time before Archimedes and Chaffinch join the Fellowship. Entry requires you to use a whole bottle of alcohol before lunch and have a desire to ~~completely give it up~~ meet other like-minded souls. There is a touch of the Freemasons about it.

Asparagus . . . Appearing at the beginning of April, plump green Asparagusses are the first major seasonal Middle Class foodie treat of the year. However, by the third week of April, having enjoyed it roasted, toasted, grilled, fried, boiled, mashed, moussed and in smoothies, we never want to see another stalk. It also has an unmentionable side effect, which can linger on well into July, and in serious cases till September, when the salmon start running.

Aldeburgh . . . On the whole, British seaside towns are not Middle Class. A rare exception is Aldborough (impossible to spell the same way twice). It's one of those places where having fish and chips in August in the driving rain is 'rather fun'. It was also the home of Benjamin ~~Brito~~ . . . ~~Britai~~ . . . Bunny, whose melody-free compositions Vintage Middlings pretend to enjoy.

ADHD . . . This is the trump card (*see* Bridge) excuse for parents of fidgety Middle Class children. In the old days, excitable offspring were beaten with a stout length of elm, now they are denied sugary snacks, which is as cruel as it is effective (not very). As for the elm trees, they have all been chopped down, so the fidgets got the last laugh.

Antiques . . . These are generally pieces of spindly brown wooden furniture. They are very easily broken or marked with rings, particularly when you are trying your hardest not to. The enduring popularity of *The Antiques Roadshow* has encouraged Middlings to believe that the pine wardrobe in the spare bedroom is an heirloom, and the rusted fire poker is The True Sword of Genghis Khan. Even Goldfinch and Cicero are in on the act, refusing to remove any toys from their boxes in case it affects their long-term value.

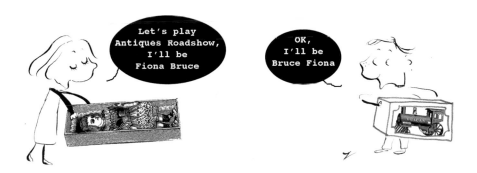

Auctions . . . A favourite Middle Class pastime is the Charity Auction. On the surface, they present philanthropically minded Middlings with the opportunity to bid for all sorts of interesting things, like snow-boarding holidays in Bulgaria and breakfast for two at a Little Chef of their choice. What they really are is an opportunity to show off in front of friends and spend spectacular sums of money on things we don't actually want. It is not until the gavel falls that we remember that we hate snow and are banned from Bulgaria for something that happened during a stag/hen weekend in the 90s. We had also actually put that money aside to pay for a ~~boob job~~ life-saving operation.

AGAs . . . The beating heart of Middle Class Britain. No one will ever question your Middle Class credentials if you are in possession of one. Invented by the Aga Khan (who is the only person rich enough to run one), AGAs are too hot to sit on and too cool to cook in. They are marvellous, however, for burning money, drying tea towels and warming pets. Despite their sturdy and reliable appearance, they are highly strung and don't cope well under pressure. In AGA households, don't expect to sit down to Christmas dinner until about teatime on Boxing Day.

luke warmth Comes out here

Money goes in here

Advent Calendars . . . There is a striking difference in taste between the generations when it comes to Advent Calendars. Older Middlings remember a time when on opening the little window, you would behold a picture of a candle or possibly a robin, which would propel you to deliriums of joy, quite overcome by Christmas fever. But for Perpetua and Zapfino, an Advent Calendar is nothing more than a rather parsimonious chocolate dispenser. They see December as the random month chosen by their parents when they are allowed to eat slightly stale chocolate before breakfast.

The Archers . . . To the Middle Class ear there is no more-reassuring sound than the theme tune to Radio 4's endless tale of framing folk (or possibly *farming* folk, we might have copied a typo from the *Radio Times*). Up and down the land, dogs and cats are fed to the dying strains of its beloved 'tum te tum' theme tune. Despite most people denying passionately that they listen to it, apply a little light torture and they will display an encyclopaedic knowledge going back years.

Arsenal . . . Middle Class men and women, with their beards and trendy glasses, are strangely attracted to Arsenal Football Club above all the others. One guesses this is entirely down to the sophisticated existential football they play and not the slightly rude nature of the team's name. We can certainly see the appeal, the ground is very well situated for a bit of tapas in Islington before the game and let's face it, you're not likely to get involved in too much argy bargy when half the supporters have their babies in slings and are wearing brogues.

Hooray Henris

Affairs . . . An inevitable problem as a result of living in such close proximity to France. Affairs are extremely exciting and arousing (apparently) right up until the moment they become legitimate, which is when they stop being Affairs, so you have to start another one. A good Middle Class Affair should involve a lot of rumpy pumpy and expeditions to places such as the amusement arcade at Weston-super-Mare, where you won't be spotted by people you know. Don't combine the two, however, or you'll get arrested (which was a nightmare and involved a lot of lying to the spouse — now ex . . .).

Alliums . . . Pert, confident and purple headed, these lollipop style floral erections are a mainstay of the Middle Class garden. Nodding sagely in a cool summer breeze, like a party of Royals at a variety show, their emergence lends a weedy border a touch of glamour. Their sophistication and air of superiority wouldn't hold quite such sway were they known by their other name, which is onions.

~~Allium~~ Onion

Alessi . . . These products can be found throughout good Middle Class households. They make lovely presents (*see* Re-Gifting) and are a perfect combination of design and fun (or irritating cuteness and uselessness, if you're in a bad mood). We find our blobby plastic toothpaste squeezers indispensable, and know of someone's aunt who adored the lime-green Alessi monkey which secured her colostomy bag in such a cheeky way, until the dog attacked it. Like all good design, Alessi proves that ~~function should follow form~~ . . . ~~form should follow function~~ . . . a last-minute Christmas shopper and his money are soon parted.

ABCs . . . Spanning Middle Class nursery walls up and down the land from Apple to Zebra. It is hard to think of anything more Middle Class than spending the day flicking through an ABC book. All those unrelated bits and bobs gathered together satisfyingly yet arbitrarily by the letter they happen to begin with. The fly in the ointment, the jeopardy which keeps you turning the pages, is what will they do when they get to X? You can't always get away with xylophone and X-ray machine. Then finally, when you've got to Z, you can go the pub . . . sorry, zoo.

Astronomy . . . No one enjoys a good gaze up at the stars more than a Middling. Flat on your back on a Tuscan terrace, a glass of Prosecco in hand. Of course, some constellations are more Middle Class than others: the Plough, the only one anyone can recognise because it looks like a heavy-bottomed saucepan, is certainly one; and Ursa Major sounds nice and military, which we like. Ryan's Belt, however . . .

7

Arthouse . . . The Middle Classes enjoy going to the cinema, but we can't survive only on the non-stop explosions and schmaltz that Hollywood sends us. We also need the more esoteric and plotless movie experience you get from low-budget and foreign films, otherwise known as Arthouse. On exiting the cinema there is usually a slightly awkward pause before someone expresses an opinion. The first to speak normally carries the rest of the party with them, but sometimes there is a dissenter in the ranks.

Allotments . . . As precious as fishing rights and these days just as Middle Class. If you want an Allotment, then it's important to take a lot of exercise, get plenty of sleep and eat your five-a-day. This is to ensure that you are still alive when you get to the front of the waiting list. Once you've finally got your Allotment, the routine of ~~growing vegetables really starts~~ sitting around drinking cider and smoking roll-ups in the potting shed with other allotmentors can really start.

Allotment

Not allotment

American-Style Fridges . . . In the vast and cavernous spaces which are the modern Middle Class kitchen, the one-up-one-down skinny British fridge-freezer looks rather white and pathetic. Thankfully, Uncle Sam, whose big-boned people know a thing or two about keeping proper quantities of victuals chilled, has come to our rescue and sent over giant, armoured, steel-plated battle fridges. They are completely bullet-proof and have cannons mounted to the front which (when they are working) fire ice ~~cubes~~ crescents across the room.

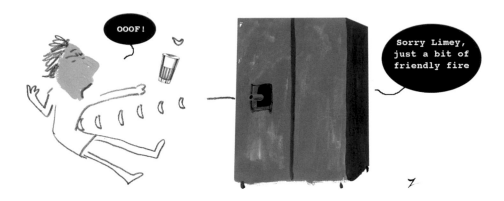

 **is for Bunting...**

Bad Backs . . . After allergies, these are the most popular Middle Class health problem. So many of us have back problems that you would almost think there was a design flaw, and humans were supposed to go around on all four paws, like our cousin the gorilla. There are all sorts of reasons why Middlings in particular suffer from Bad Backs, including the wearing of brogues, sitting in draughts on inherited furniture, moving pianos, bunting-hanging and having picnics.

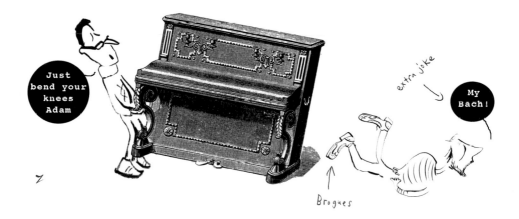

Blackboards . . . Since the invention of blackboard paint, Middlings, particularly those with chicks in the nest, have been unable to resist the urge to slap it onto their kitchen walls. This has a twofold effect on the atmosphere, simultaneously bringing forth memories of the school-room and the gastropub, which makes most of us feel very happy. Blackboards, of course, have long been appropriated by the bossy for the pronouncement of their latest orders or extracts from their manifestos. If you suffer from endless instructions displayed in this way, then simply replace the chalk with its polar opposite, cheese.

Bags for Life . . . It's quite a responsibility to take on a Bag for Life, life can last a very long time these days and many of them are only woven from twisted moss, string and twigs. In reality, it's not such a problem as they're not likely to be used more than once. Most of us forget to put them back in the car when we go shopping and have to buy new ones every time we go to the supermarket.

Books . . . Before eBooks came along, Books were annoying papery things that got in the way, with their silly covers and that smell . . . of Books. One thing we do hope eBooks will never replace are those lovely big picture Books Middlings like to leave on their coffee tables but never ever read.

Barbeques . . . There are two essentials of Barbecuing. One is that it is an entirely male activity, and the other is you must try to burn the meat on the outside and leave it bloody on the inside, especially if it is chicken. If you have a foodie amongst your guests, for heaven's sake tell them that the meat has been marinating for days. Despite the three-legged, black, UFO-type Barbeque being an almost perfect design, some Middlings have been acquiring vast gas-powered outdoor kitchen ranges. Not only do these cost an arm and a leg (of lamb, butterflied) but they take up half the garden and don't burn the meat properly.

Bird Feeders . . . We Middlings love our feathered friends, and what better way to enjoy a pair of Great Tits up close than to dangle some nut bags in front of the kitchen window. The art of Bird Feeding is getting more sophisticated all the time; we now know that Goldfinches like niger seed, Bluetits like fat balls and Robins like Datman.

Budget Airlines . . . These days the highlight of most Middle Class holidays is how ghastly the flight was. Flid airport was actually two hundred miles from Flid, in Flob, a €300 taxi fare away. Horatio had not paid the surcharge for Asparagus to have a suitcase and he had to cough up a €280 excess. It was revealed that his wife was pregnant when airport security put her through the full body X-ray machine, so he had to buy another ticket for the embryo. In the end, it would have been cheaper to charter a Learjet, but not so Middle Class . . . or fun.

Brunch . . . Middlings are only just starting to get the hang of Brunch, or Bruncheon, as it is more properly called. It was originally called *lunchfast*, but everyone got indigestion. It was invented by big-boned Americans as a meal to keep them going between breakfast and lunch. Being more parsimonious, we Middlings think of it as an opportunity to save money by *combining* the two. We particularly enjoy chicken porridge or boiled eggs with lamb ~~soldiers~~ shoulders, all washed down by coffee with salad cream in it.

BBC Four . . . For Vintage Middlings, BBC Four, like Viagra, is one of the few things that makes progress seem worthwhile. For even though they have barely cocked a glance at the other 900 channels, they turn with gleeful anticipation to BBC Four to enjoy a documentary about iron bridges in the West Midlands. They know it's naughty because it's telly, but it is not *so* bad because they are learning something. All in all, it's rather like using organic crack as opposed to the regular muck . . . but not quite as moreish.

Boutique Hotels . . . Warning! It is *not* Middle Class to stay in a hotel anymore, we should only use Boutique Hotels. There is no discernible difference, apart from the price, the pattery wallpaper, the fact that the bath is often parked right in the middle of your room, there are button-backed sofas everywhere and a heady waft of Leaf de Fig from one of the many scented candles around the place. In fact, we can now see why they're so expensive, carry on.

Hotel   Boutique Hotel

The good news is I've run you a bath, the bad news is your suitcase was in the bath..

Board Games . . . Despite the fact that Mulberry and Squirrel would far rather mess about on their mobile phones, we are convinced that a game of Monopoly will be more wholesome and an excellent way of teaching them the importance of getting on the property ladder, the value of money and getting credit, at a young age. However, it does mean that they see a weaker side of *our* characters, as we cheat and lie in a vain attempt not to pay the rent on a hotel in Mayfair to a 7-year-old. And as for Scrabble, only the most stable of families should ever attempt it. After inheritances, it is the single most divisive activity and creates lifelong feuds. The addition of a strategically placed B is all it takes to turn a happy *union* into a *bunion* (and it only scores you 12 points).

Beaches . . . Rather like a bath, a Beach is either too hot, too cold or too full of jellyfish. Remember to put sun cream on absolutely everything at least twice an hour, especially your eBook and your hair. Sandwiches wouldn't be proper sandwiches without the liberal addition of sand. Some beaches are not sandy but pebbly, and if you are having sandwiches on a pebbly beach then make sure you have a dentist in your party.

Boxed Sets . . . We Modern Middlings don't like being pinned down at the same hour each week to watch our favourite telly shows; we are far too busy pruning the bunting, going to Carluccio's and whatforth. Thankfully, Boxed Sets exist to make waiting about for the week to pass moribund. They look harmless enough sitting in the box, but pop one in your DVD machine and you'll find they are far more addictive than crack-balls.

Ballet . . . Despite no discernible enthusiasm, it is important for Zephyr and Puffin – once they are walking – to be put in tutus and driven to Ballet Class. Thudding about a sports hall for an hour a week is one of the first Middle Class rites of passage. It should in most cases lead to a lifelong dislike of Ballet, which will save a lot of money. Of the Middlings who do fall in love with Ballet, it is normally the females who are most likely to visit a loan shark and buy tickets for the Royal Balletdrome. It is worth noting that this has *nothing* to do with the fact that male ballerinas can get very hungry and keep spare sandwiches in their tights next to their ding dongs.

Beekeeping . . . Thank goodness there is an increasing number of Middlings choosing to keep bees. Bee numbers are in dangerous decline, and when there are no bees left, the entire planetary iosystem will e uggered . . .

B&Bs . . . Once Marmalade and Poodle have gone to uni (university), their bedrooms should be stripped of pony posters, porn and Arsenal team photos. Everything that remains should be painted French Grey. Next, buy some eggs and bacon from the nearest petrol station (locally sourced) and you are now ready to open up your house as a B&B. This is a win-win, as during the holidays you can charge Marmalade and Poodle 'mates rates' to rent their old rooms back.

Book Club . . . There is nothing more uplifting in Middle Class Britain than a room full of middle-aged Middlings discussing *Middlemarch*. For many members of Book Clubs, it is much more than an exploration of mere plot and theme . . .

Balsamic Vinegar . . . Invented by the rather soft and wooden Irishman Balsa Mick, this vinegar, appropriated like everything foodie by the Italians, has transformed the Middle Class salad. Like most things in life, you get what you pay for (unless you're buying a flight on a budget airline), and the more you spend the better (thicker and sweeter) the Balsamic. If Jack falls down and breaks his crown, for heaven's sake take him to A&E, don't waste the Balsamic and brown paper on him.

Bridge . . . Not the BBC Four special but the drinking game beloved of Middlings since its invention by Isambard Kingdom Brunel in 1066. It requires four Middlings to sit around a square table and get very drunk while shuffling cards, making random statements and trumping. The drunkest person becomes a 'dummy', misses his turn and has to mix the drinks for the others until he sobers up a bit. At the end, everyone empties their pockets, hand their spare change and car keys to each other, before going upstairs and having an orgy.

Blazers . . . Surely the most affecting sartorial sight in Middle Class Britain today is the Middling male in his prime (about sixty), in navy Blazer with brightwork buttons, appearing against a pink sky in Salcombe. We can't write any more on the subject, we are quite overcome.

us, overcome

Bloody . . . Bloody hell! Bloody bugger! Bloody Mary! These are some Bloody good Middle Class expletives. You can use *Bloody* in pretty much any situation other than a scene where there actually is lot of blood, such as a nosebleed. To say 'My goodness, that's a Bloody Bloody nose you've got there!' would be confusing, and it might be more helpful to proffer a hanky. A Bloody Mary is the favourite Middling drink of a Sunday morning. We take it in the mistaken belief that it is a cure for hangovers (like the Loch Ness Monster, there is no such thing). In fact it just gets you drunk again, which in the short term is a Bloody relief.

Boden . . . In the old days the expression for being sartorially with-it was 'à la mode', for today's Middlings it is 'à la Bode'. From its moleskin suits to its very fun prints, the Boden catalogue has been soft porn for a generation of Middling mums, and its founder, Johnnie Boden (Johnnie, if you don't know him), is our Peter Stringfellow. If you have ever bought anything from Boden you will find that you have to actually move house to get away from the catalogues which keep cascading through your letterbox every week.

Bats . . . Apart from the terror most Middle Class women experience when stuck in a room with a Bat — that he will ~~take human form, attach himself to her neck and suck thirstily on her blood~~ touch her hair — we are all rather fond of Bats. There is a rule that you have to say, 'Oh look, a Bat!' whenever you see one. This is usually a sign that you have stayed too long at a barbeque party. Recently, Middlings have discovered a new use for Bats, and that is in thwarting planning permission for the neighbours' Scandinavian-style live/work garden office. If you can prove that any particularly unusual Bats are enjoying the chilly thermals above your cottage of an evening, then the game is literally up.

Bread-Making Machines . . . The problem with today's enormous Middle Class kitchens is all the spare workspace. Thankfully, some bright spark came to the rescue and invented the Bread-making Machine. They are designed to be used once and then left on the side, pushed up against the wall, next to the yoghurt weaver, wheatgrass blender, carrot juicer and café equipment.

Bread maker

Brogues . . . There is something bunting-twitchingly Middle Class about a pair of Brogues. Like crumpets, but in leather. It is so reassuring, on looking down, to be greeted by a constellation of little holes smiling back at you. They have been worn for ever by rural Middlings, but the fashion for wearing them in *town* was encouraged by Mr Silly, Mr Noisy and later on by Mr Tall. It is advisable when wearing Brogues to put one on *each* foot, the rogue Brogue is not in vogue.

Bugaboos . . . There are three big purchases in your life: your house, your car and your ~~divorce~~ buggy. The biggest of these is your buggy, and the most Middle Class must'ave buggy (despite sounding like an act of sodomy performed on a ghost) is the Bugaboo. They have done to buggies what Dyson did to hoovers, that is to say, made them very colourful, plastic, expensive and tricky to assemble, all with the intention of making babies (like hoovering) appealing to men. It has worked.

Belfast Sinks . . . What ~~comes~~ goes around ~~goes comes~~ goes around, and no mistake! When we were young (in the late nineteenth century) Belfast Sinks were all the rage. Hard, white tubs that were perfect for washing the children, pigs and pewter plates in. Gradually, however, in the days we now refer to as 'The Belfast Troubles', china crockery caught on, which smashed to pieces as soon as it so much as brushed against the side of a Belfast Sink. So we ripped them all out, put them in the corners of fields for cows to kick, and replaced them with stainless-steel sinks with built-in grooves for drainage. Time, however, is a healer (not for my Great Uncle Snuffbox, though; he got killed when a station clock fell on his head) and now Middlings are back in love with the Belfast Sink and the sound of broken crockery can be heard up and down the land once again. And this, patient reader, is the reason why Emma Bridgewater makes such thick mugs and plates.

Brabantia Bins . . . Only a Middling could take something as unpromising as a bin and make it a Middle Class must'ave. Before Brabantias came along, we used to hide our bins in cupboards. Now we let them stand proudly in the corner of the kitchen, like chrome pillar boxes. Press the chin and the mouth opens. They're very clever and in fact some of the best conversations we've had at drunken parties have been with the Brabantia Bin.

Bicycle Seats . . . To observe, from the safety of a pavement café, a Middling Mummy or Daddy wobbling along on their bicycle with darling Beelzebub balanced precariously on the back, while heading out into the oncoming traffic, is one of modern life's most alarming sights. It is even more dangerous than a blindfolded man throwing knives at his wife strapped to a revolving wheel, but strangely not as entertaining.

Blogging . . . In the far-off times, when filing cabinets had brass handles, many Middlings would keep a journal. They kept these writings extremely private, the thought of anyone reading them until they were long dead was, in most cases, anathema. Then the monks at Tinternet Abbey in Wales invented the Internet, everyone went celebrity mad and suddenly we all started Blogging our private goings-on for all and sundae to read. Apparently, this is a particular problem in the Amazon Rainforest, which is very bad for the ecosystem and must be curtailed.

Basildon Bond . . . Great uncle to James Bond, but like Tonbridge Wells and Quality Street, not very fashionable anymore. In fact, it is so unfashionable you can buy it at the Post Office. However, it was once the writing paper of choice for the Middle Classes. If we remember rightly, it was pale blue and rather too small; the classy bit was the watermark, which as children we ~~stupidly~~ charmingly thought said 'Basil Brush'.

 is for Complaining...

Charities . . . Because being Middle Class is so much fun, we all feel a little guilty that we're not suffering like the Not at all Posh or the Properly Posh do. This guilt drives us into the arms of the Charities. We furiously sign up for standing orders until we have more money leaving our accounts and going to developing countries, disaster zones, homeless owls and donkey sanctuaries each month than is actually coming in.

Christmas Shopping . . . As Oscar Fry once said, 'By the time you're bored of Christmas, it'll nearly be November' (we're not sure what he meant, but it's clearly terribly witty). One of the most irritating things about Christmas for Middlings is the early appearance of decorations in shops. In very bad years this overlaps with the summer sales, but generally you can only expect to shop in a tinsel-free environment until the end of August. In the old days we used to die of consumption, now it just gives us sore arms.

a bad case of consumption

Christmas Plans . . . 'What are we doing about Christmas this year?' This is a question, normally asked towards the end of the summer holiday, that strikes fear into Middle Class hearts. Taking into account the dynamics of the modern Middling family renders Christmas impossible to arrange to everyone's satisfaction. Achilles and Goldilocks have six sets of grandparents, all of whom expect to see them. As a result most Christmases are spent in the car.

Christmas Dinner . . . If the answer to the question, 'What are we doing about Christmas this year?' is, 'Spend it at *your* house', then you have to face the next dilemma: turkey or goose? At some point someone will chip in helpfully with, 'In the old days people ate beef', but turkey and goose, as everyone knows, are the only real runners in a two-~~horse~~ bird race. The fact that a goose can only, at a stretch, feed four should have some bearing on the outcome of this debate. So now you've decided on a turkey, what can possibly go wrong?

Clementines . . . For a month every year (December) in a bid to avoid (common) colds, Middlings binge on vitamin C taken in the shape (round) of small oranges. They used to be called tangerines or satsumas, but now they are known by the more Middle Class name of Clementines. People sometimes question our assertion that Clementines are more Middle Class than tangerines and we reply, 'Well, do you think Winston Churchill would have married someone called tangerine?', which shuts them up.

Christmas Cards . . . Every winter the British Middle Class pulls together and tries to do its bit to keep the Post Office in business by posting Christmas Cards to everyone we've ever met. Sending them is definitely not as much fun as receiving them. You should always hope to receive as many as you've posted, if not more, and it is important to share your popularity by displaying your cards prominently. We normally send ourselves quite a few just to pad it out, but it is important to buy a variety of designs so as to outwit suspicious visitors.

Cupcakes . . . American people quite often call each other 'Cupcake', which, if we're honest, isn't very nice of them. For what is a Cupcake? A crinkled paper case filled with a dollop of sponge topped with a sickly coating. Had Marie Antoinette declared, as the people protested beneath her window, 'Let them eat Cupcakes', there would have been a revolution! At some Middle Class weddings the wedding cake must get dropped, because in its place is a pile of Cupcakes, which presumably the bride's mother had to whip up at the last minute. We all say 'Cupcakes, what fun!' But deep down it's very disappointing.

Countryside Alliance . . . This is a club for Middlings who wear Wellington boots but actually *do* live in the country. They love animals, but understanding that nature is cruel, know that sometimes they have to kill them too. If it wasn't for the Countryside Alliance, the landscape of Britain would be a right old jungle, populated by marauding herds of foxes, squirrels and paintballers with not a proper Land Rover in sight. A ghastly thought.

Cornwall . . . Its bracing winds, stinging rain, tiny lanes and jellyfish make this the ideal place for a Middling to spend a few weeks every summer for their *second* holiday. On the down side, the rental cottages are too small for the amount of Middlings we try to cram in and the hot water can only stretch to one bath, two inches deep, per day. On the plus side, if your marriage can survive a week in Cornwall it can survive *anything* and the pubs do still hum with the oaths of seadogs, smugglers, tin miners, pasty makers, fishermen and artists. Only *very* occasionally, above their charming chatter, will you hear the ~~braying~~ dulcet tones of Agamemnon telling Chutney how much better the weather was in Positano.

Compost . . . Every Middle Class household has its own rules on what can and cannot enter through the portals of the Compost Bucket into the hereafter, the Compost Heap. The nemesis of the good compostier are rats. 'NO EGG SHELLS in the Compost, Agrippa, the *rats!*' is the cry in one home, while in another it is, 'Fred, NO HUMAN REMAINS in the Compost, the *rats* will come back!' More care is taken dispensing with the leftovers than with preparing the food in the first place, and most Middlings move house (to escape the Boden catalogues) before their precious Compost is ready to use anyway.

Chocolate . . . Chocolate is a delicious way to show off your Middle Class credentials. If you are a planet-friendly, eco-saving, Afro-Caribbean Middling then Green & Black's will be for you. For the jet set there is nothing that says, 'I've been through an airport' more clearly than an enormous Toblerone. For the rest of us there are cocoa solids to count. Some Chocolates, like KitKats and Mars Bars, are classless, but any boxes of Chocolate bought from petrol stations are not Middle Class unless they've been disguised to look like something else, i.e., the mighty Chocolate Orange or the Praline Seashells, both of which are a hell of a lot of fun.

Cocaine . . . Cocaine is a very expensive coffee substitute found on the backs of porcelain lavatory cisterns at racy Middle Class dinner parties. Lazy Middlings often call it 'coke' like the popular fizzy cola drink, which can lead to hilarious misunderstandings when, for instance, a child asks for some coke and you hand them a rolled-up fiver. The bemused look on Bodkin's face is priceless, unless of course he snatches it up and totters off to the loo, which would be worrying.

Crocs . . . Crocs are a plastic shoe-cum-colander much favoured by Middlings who can't ~~grow up~~ get the hang of flip-flops. They are available in all sizes, the little ones being relatively harmless, but do approach the larger adult sizes with extreme caution.

Cider . . . Once only found in 5-litre containers and drunk by farmers and schoolchildren until they were sick, it has of late reversed the force of gravitation (sorry Newton) and re-ascended the class ladder. It really is beyond doubt that it may be used in cooking or to put out a fire with impunity. If you insist on actually drinking it then a tiny amount used to fill in the gaps in a glassful of ice is the safest way to enjoy it.

Cleaners . . . Hiring a Cleaner is an important step in establishing yourself as Middle Class. Once you have one, it is important that you complain endlessly about how useless they are to anyone who will listen. Paying them is an awful bore; they only take cash, which of course you never have quite enough of. They also leave lists of incredibly specific stuff for you to buy, like kitchen cupboard hinge degunge spray, which costs the earth. Try to avoid getting into conversations with your Cleaner. Their life will be both more interesting and more boring than yours. And never patronise them as most Cleaners, you will find, also have Cleaners of their own.

Cashmere . . . Or 'mere cash', if you like to split words in half and reverse their order. Coincidentally it *is* mere cash which separates the lambswool wearer from the sporter of Cashmere. It was, of course, invented by the great crooning country music softie Johnny Cashmere, The Man in Black (and usually V-neck) Cashmere. Much to the delight of the clothes moth, Middlings are rather overdoing it with the whole Cashmere thing. You can now get Cashmere oven gloves, Cashmere bin bags and even Cashmere bunting.

Cotswolds . . . The rolling wolds with their honey-coloured villages and well-managed bunting are to a Middling what the shallow end of a public swimming pool is to a paedophile. They come alive (grind to a halt) at the weekend, when the lanes are blocked with the sort of vehicles you would expect to see outside The Casino in Monte Carlo. The farm shops are better stocked with celebrity cheeses than Harrods, and three out of four people in the pub you recognise from the telly. There are few prouder moments in a Middle Class life than when you have finally exchanged on a cottage in the Poshwolds and you walk up your garden path saying, 'It's not much, but I like to call it my second home.'

Cheese . . . It is widely known that the British now make more varieties of Cheese than the French. Quantity does not necessarily mean quality, however, as most of these Cheeses are made by Middlings who have moved to the country and just thought it would be a fun thing to do. The big Middle Class Cheese conundrum is still what do you do with the leftover Stilton after Christmas? We remain convinced that Stilton and brocolli soup is another name for gangrene.

Camper Vans . . . Middle Class couples who fancy pushing their marriages to the brink but can't afford a week in Cornwall find that the next best thing is a Camper Van. The opportunities to argue are unparalleled, and to make matters more exciting there is absolutely no escaping each other, unless you run out of petrol, which happens suspiciously often.

Chickens . . . Ever since the intrusion of 'best before' dates on eggshells, Middlings have flocked (this is not the joke) to buy live Chickens ~~to decorate the garden with~~ from which to get our own unmarked eggs. We know exactly what to look for in a good Chicken. It is not the size of the eggs or even the regularity of the laying, but the fluffiness of its feet and the tuftiness of its head.

Croquet . . . Only inheritances or possibly board games are a more effective way of destroying the bonds that bind the Middle Class family than Croquet. Knowing this does not in any way dull our enthusiasm for the sport; if anything, it sharpens it. For the full effect, play it slightly drunk and near an apple tree with an angry wasps' nest in it. The Croquet mallet is ideally shaped for bashing in heads, and remember – every family has its own rules . . .

Coffee . . . The reason that real Coffee has triumphed over instant is not because it tastes better but because it comes with far more kit, and we Middlings love our kit. At the very least, we are all in possession of several cafetières, an aluminium flip-lid hob top, a bean grinder, a café-style espresso machine, some tiny cups (which *we* always thought were for mulled sherry), a frappuccino whisk and some paper filters at the bottom of the clingfilm drawer. The only advantage of the collapse of the high street has been the rise in the number of Coffeehouses. You can bounce off the wall of one and straight through the door of another.

Clouds . . . It is very Middle Class to know the Latin names of different Cloud varieties. Most Middlings know *fluffius stringius* and *puffius looks like rainius*, but you would be considered something of a nerd if you professed to know any more than that. It is quite fun to lie on your back after a picnic (before you pack away the bunting), look up at the sky and try to see familiar things in the Clouds. Popular Middle Class Cloud spottings include Churchill puffing on a cigar, Alan Titchmarsh pruning dahlias and Delia Smith stuffing a turkey. The ultimate sighting is all six Mitford sisters playing sardines.

Crabs . . . Crabs are a lot of fun, from the dangle-baiting that Middle Class children do off jetties in Cornwall and Norfolk to the bashing of the shells and teasing out of claw flesh. They are considered by female Middlings to be a snack of the highest *hors d'oeuvre*, but no males understand this because (rather like with chicken) it is the females who get to eat the delicious strands of gorgeous white flesh while they get the brown sloppy brains and intestines and are considered awful wimps if they don't grin and bear it.

> Bravo Aubergina! Daddy can kill it and cook it and we can feast on the firm white flesh and he can have all the brown goo he loves so much

Crumpets . . . When ex-pat Middlings start to think about Crumpets they actually weep tears of melted butter, because, of course, Crumpets are unavailable outside Britain. Wonderfully, they remind us of the nursery, even if we've never been in one in our lives. There is nothing sexist about a crumpet; in fact it is considered a great compliment for a hot woman to be called a 'Nice bit of Crumpet'. In short, they are a true cornerstone of Middle Class Britain (which is possibly why it tilts a bit to the left).

Center Parcs . . . If you will insist on taking Spitfire, Pashmina and Firkin on a triathlon holiday (cycling, swimming and eating) in a British wood, then your best bet would be a Center Parc. Left behind by aliens in the 1980s in woodlands all over Britain, they have all the advantages of normal woodlands apart from the fact that they are encased in domes of weather-proof glass. And so, like Little Red Riding Hood, you can wander about to your heart's content, even after darc.

Country Life (Magazine, not Butter) . . . This weekly glossy used to be about countryside pursuits, but, rather like the real countryside, today it's all about property and swag curtains. That is, for the first fifty pages; thereafter it's all girls in pearls, a cartoon about dogs and AGAs and a few pages about a very interesting clock which hasn't been seen since the 1970's. Rather like with *The Lady* magazine, no amount of propaganda telling us that *Country Life* has been radically modernised will convince us that it actually has been, and a good thing too.

Chelsea Flower Show . . . Obviously every village in London has its own flower show, but Chelsea's is the biggest. It offers a wonderful opportunity for Middlings to huddle together under enormous umbrellas and try to catch a glimpse of Alan Titchmarsh and other ~~vaguely irritating celebrities~~ national treasures, who stagger around oohing and aahing at various 'gardens' of polished steel and plywood. The main object of the show appears to be to remind us how lucky we are to have the gardens that we *do* have, and to remind us what could happen if they were unfortunate enough to win the lottery and then feel the need to employ a cutting-edge garden designer.

Regular flower

Chelsea flower

Cats . . . Apart from songbirds, dogs, mice, baby rabbits and people who are allergic to them, we are, as a nation, in love with the Cat. If you have one then the best thing to do with it is to sit down and let it sprawl across your lap. Thus positioned with a happy purring Cat, you become exempt from any jobs such as cooking supper, putting out the recycling or paying the TV licence (this might have been a one-off). As a nation we actually spend more annually on Cat Calendars than we do on defence (no idea if this is true, but we think it probably is).

Careers . . . These are something Middlings are absolutely expected to have. We climb up Career Ladders, we dash down Career Paths, we even leave our children during their formative years in the dubious company of the au pair while we nurture our precious Careers. Then suddenly we drop the whole thing and career off to the Poshwolds to make cheese.

Cushions . . . Middlings tend towards two different types of Cushion. There are the old ones, built of sturdy stuff, which never really age or look out of place. And there are the new ones. These are usually given as presents and tend to be rather fun. Cushion fashion changes as often as the weather. It wasn't that long ago that medieval tapestry unicorns were all the rage (but not much fun); now fun reigns in the shape of bold patterns, Union Jacks, slogans and even biscuits. Worryingly, there is a trend, started in hotels and embraced by Middlings, for putting Cushions on beds. This is clearly daft and any ornaments that get smashed when the Cushions are flung off are frankly asking for it.

Car Stickers . . . Like Grand Prix drivers, many Middlings enjoy decorating their vehicles with the logos of organisations to which they are affiliated: National Trust, RSPB, Poppies, Help for Heroes, Wildlife Trust, RNLI, Countryside Alliance, to name but six. It is a harmless way of showing the world who you are and what you believe in. Unlike Grand Prix drivers, however, there is a rule that the more stickers that festoon your car the slower you will drive. Whether this is a deliberate ploy to give others the time to read them or merely a direct consequence of the added weight and wind drag to the vehicle is not clear. They are also not a huge help when parallel parking.

Cachepots . . . These are highly sophisticated Middle Class accessories, the purpose of which is to hide unsightly flowerpots. More than that, they are a beacon that shows just how far humanity, as a species, has come. French people of a certain age remember growing up to a wonderful animated television caper called *Guillaume et Benjamin les Cache-Pots Hommes*. In the parlours of Europe they completely eclipsed our own rather crude Bill and Ben.

Colour Supplements . . . The sole purpose of the Colour Supplement appears to be to make the Middling feel wretched about their lot. When we have finally finished paying the last instalment on our granite and zinc kitchen and are relaxing in it after bruncheon with a Bloody Mary, innocently flicking through the supplements, what do we get but an article by a designer telling us that granite and zinc kitchens are sooo yesterday; the cool cats are cooking in kitchens made from varnished Weetabix where each drawer plays a different tune upon opening (actually, quite a good idea). Then there's a smug fellow who bought the entire Dalmatian coast for six hundred quid in 2004 and is now the twelfth richest man in Britain. Next there's a perfect family who have a gypsy caravan in their meadow-style garden; their children have the same names as ours, but are better looking. Just before we explode the last thing we see is an advert for an enormous watch.

Cricket . . . Cricket is another popular Middle Class drinking game. You have wine before you start, then squash, then tea, then finally beer, lots and lots of beer. This is why all Cricket pitches have a public lavatory next to them. Charmingly, this is referred to as the pavilion. For female Middlings, watching their menfolk playing Cricket is a bit of a bore. The Sunday papers blow away, the children and dogs run on to the pitch and the other wives are awful bitches. It really isn't Cricket.

Crème Fraîche . . . One reason that the environs of French patisseries are not piled high with the corpses of heart-attack victims is that they use Crème Fraîche rather than double cream in their cakework. Middlings, who are also partial to the odd millefeuille or profiterole pyramid, have clocked this and sales of the healthier and ever so slightly sour crème fraîche now exceed those of double cream (we have no idea if this is actually true). There is something sly about Crème Fraîche, however; it holds something back, like a cat, while double cream is more like a dog.

Châteaux . . . Most Middlings who buy property in France buy a Château. At least that's what they like to think. If you speak to their neighbours, they would reveal that the 'Château' prior to its purchase by the Boden-Jones was in fact a perfectly normal farmhouse. The new owners insisted that a pointy cone was put on the chimney and then boastfully rebranded it a Château. This is all very well until they try and light a fire, or the locals get round to having another revolution, in which case the Boden-Jones will be amongst the first for the choppeau.

Corkscrews . . . The reason we have so many Corkscrews is that they are a perfect last-minute Christmas present. It is impossible for a Middling to possess fewer than a dozen different types. Normally, the more expensive and extravagant – the less effective. You must not admit this, of course, when you emerge from the pantry clasping the latest titanium Corktug Sportif and clamp it to a bottle, then struggle for an hour before you realise that the last cork you removed is still attached to the curly bit and you're deuced if you can get it out. We read an interesting report in *Corkscrewer World* the other day saying that screw tops are actually no good for wine, tainting the flavour, which is a shame as they offered such hope.

I'm terribly sorry waiter but this wine is screwed

Cookery Books . . . One of the reasons we have such enormous kitchens is to house our vast libraries of Cookery Books. Despite this, we have the same problem squeezing our latest acquisition into the shelf as we do squeezing our own bulging middles into our trousers, which is a direct consequence of the former. Occasionally, along comes a must'ave Cookery Book, such as Nutella Lawson's *I'm on Heat* or Jamie O'Liver's *Bish Bosh Nosh*, and you will be given three or four copies of each for Christmas. It is a comfort knowing we have so many Cookery Books we can turn to, in a power cut with a torch, when tiresomely we can't look up the recipe we want on the internet.

Corduroy . . . Tweed, linen and Corduroy: the Holey (if you wear them too much) Trinity of Middle Class Fabrics. The word is derived from cord (twined material) du (*of* in French) and Roy, a not very Middle Class man's name. In short: Roy's trousers. Of course this isn't strictly true, Corduroy trousers are just the start of it; you can get suits, skirts, shirts and yurts all made in Corduroy. It is particularly popular in country areas, where Middlings can recognise kindred souls, and from the cord count know if a village pub is safe to enter.

Carluccios . . . Where once Middlings flocked to Pizza Express, now their high streatery of choice is Carluccios. In the same way that McDonalds has Ronald McDonald, Carluccios has a cartoon character called Antonio who staggers about kissing his fingers like an Italian. There are so many children and prams in Carluccios that many people believe it, incorrectly, to be a chain of crèches. The children are actually dwarves who are paid to be there to give you that elusive Italian family feel.

Conservatories . . . In the olden days when orange juice was served on a doily as a starter and Protestants persecuted Catholics, little hidden rooms were created in attics to hide the priests and were called 'Priest's Holes'. In the early twenty first century, when the Labours ruled the land and the Tories were on the run, people would build cheap plastic greenhouses on the sides of their houses to hide them in; they were called 'Conserve a Torys'. They weren't very effective, being completely see-through, and most of the Tories were rounded up and made to apologise for the sleaze they had perpetrated. We forgave them, and these days the Tories are back in Westminster and Middlings use their conservatories for storing their nastiest wicker furniture.

Crudités . . . The sight of a floral Portmeirion platter carefully arranged with batons of raw vegetables and a ramekin of dip will only get the most traditional Middle Class heart racing. These days it's all about chorizo and parmesan poppadoms, and the healthy sound of a stick of celery being crunched is only heard on a Sunday morning when Tuscany's finished her third Bloody Mary and is hinting that she's just about ready for some lunch. Nowadays Crudités are only found in children's lunch boxes, put in hopefully by parents and ignored by Timon and Cadmium.

Charades . . . Most Middling hearts sink at the suggestion of Charades after dinner, but through forced smiles we find ourselves saying, 'Charades, oh yes, what fun!' It quickly escalates into a viciously competitive battle, and all dignity is abandoned to the good of the team as we find ourselves simulating masturbation in an attempt to convey the 'sounds like' of the third and fourth syllables of *Casablanca*.

Chutney . . . The alchemy of turning unwanted fruits and vegetables into pickled preserves, thence decanted into recycled jam jars (with only small fragments of the previous label remaining, despite furious finger nail agitations), which can be given as presents or stacked indefinitely in the larder is an example of Middle Class perfection. There isn't much that boiled for hours in vinegar, won't turn into Chutney, from grass clippings and unsold ABC books, all the way to missing persons.

You seem very keen on making chutney. Is it any good?

Oh yes Officer, people die for it!

Capability Brown . . . The man who dispensed with precision and formality in the garden and a great inspiration to Middle Class gardeners, particularly those who can't afford a gardener and don't care much for weeding. He popularised the landscape style of rolling lawny vistas interspersed with clumps of trees and curved lakes. His Romantic pastoral vision is ideal if you have a few hundred acres to play with, but not so good if you are restricted to a window box and a couple of grow-bags. Don't let this prevent you deploying his lessons in other parts of the house, however . . .

table laid in the style of 'Capability' Brown

Courses . . . If proof were required that Middle Class Britain is practically Utopia, you need look no further than our fondness for Courses. In his book ~~Uttoxeter~~ *Utopia*, Sir Thomas More suggested that learning new skills would replace conventional relaxational activities such as drinking and fighting. In modern Middle Class Britain his fancies are realised. No subject is too obscure to have a Course in it. Everything from bunting folding to grave digging is available, and if you ever find yourself a bit short, then hosting a Course of your own is the obvious solution. (See application form in back of book for week-long residential Course in how to write an ABC book. Only £2,000 per person – cash only, breakfast (continental) included.)

Chorizo . . . Despite an uncertainty with its pronunciation, Middlings can't get enough of this spicy orange sausage. The addition of it to any dish is pretty sure to ~~completely take it over~~ nicely enhance it. The craze started in gastropubs, where it was paired successfully with absolutely everything, and it has now spread as far as the Orkneys and even parts of Norfolk. The brown milk caused by Coco Pops is a distant memory; these days Pellegrino and Oxbridge delight in the orange sausagey milk generated by their daily bowl of Cheerizios.

D is for Dictionaries...

Deslyxia . . . If you can spell it, you haven't got it . . . but your children still might.

Dogs . . . As the famous saying goes, 'You can't teach an old sleeping ~~Dog~~ man's best friend for life and not just ~~new tricks~~ for Christmas!', so it's no surprise that Middlings are generally so fond of them. It is part of the Middle Class dream: the house in the Poshwolds, the Heritage Vegetable Garden and the Dog. In the old days people would give their Dogs the names they really wanted to give their children but weren't quite brave enough; these days it's the other way round and it's the Dogs who are called Dave and Colin and the children Caesar and Piddles.

Dinner Parties . . . Since we smashed down our dining-room walls to make our kitchens bigger, Dinner Parties now take place in the kitchen. If you aren't invited to lots of them, then you probably wish you were, and if you *are* then you wish you could just have a quiet night in. They are much less formal than they used to be, what with sitting soft (on the sofa) and sitting hard (outside on a bench), but they still offer endless opportunities for showing off and fauxing pas. The biggest faux pas is being boring, which drives most guests to drink too much which results in the next biggest faux pas, ~~vomiting all over the table~~ knocking your glass over.

Diets . . . Having crossed great bellies of pork and navigated seas of crème anglaise at a hundred kitchen suppers, understandably many Middlings feel inclined to Diet. The best Diet is one where you can eat whatever you want, but these don't normally work so well. There are plenty of others to choose from, but rather like cookery books, it is to the latest that we turn in the vain hope that one has finally been invented that actually works. Many of them are very antisocial, but the more inconvenience the Diet will cause other people, the better; after all, a trouble (or a doughnut) shared is a trouble halved.

Dorset or Devon . . . Gay or straight, chicken or salmon, colostomy bag or Dignitas; sometimes as a Middling we have decide one way or another. Obviously the cream teas are better in Devon, but in Dorset you are more likely to run over a celebrity chef. Dorset has Corfe Castle, but Devon has the Blackpool Tower . . . you do the maths (and the geography).

Drugs . . . Apart from the very hardcore types of Drugs, such as methylated crack balls, crystal acid and Nurofen Plus, Drugs have successfully insinuated themselves into Middle Class life. Almost all grown-up Middlings have taken them, but it breaks our hearts to think of our own sweet Zeus and Paprika getting off their faces. Magic mushrooms tick the most Middle Class boxes, as they are found by foraging, which makes them organic, seasonal *and* you have to put on your wellies to go for a walk to find them (see one of Psychedelia Smith's many books for recipes).

Dualit toasters . . . When these semi-industrial clockwork toasters first appeared we Middlings couldn't believe our luck. Originally intended for use in schools and hospitals, early models were hampered by the slimness of their slots, which would allow only cheap sliced white to enter. When doorstops of homemade wholemeal Middle Class bread were forced in, they could then not be extracted, leading to small bonfires taking hold inside the toaster, which in turn set off our smoke alarms. They were soon given a Middle Class makeover, including slot-widening and ticker muffling, but the fact remains that you can still buy seventeen conventional toasters, three loaves of bread and a tub of spreadable Lurpak for the price of one Dualit. Crumbs!

Dordogne . . . With its markets and honey-coloured villages, the Dordogne reminds us of the Poshwolds before it filled up with celebrities. Technically it's in France, but don't waste time mustering up your best French and asking for 'Deux pastis silver plait' in a quaint village bar. Your request will be met by the plummy tones of the innkeeper saying, 'Don't I recognise you from Oxford?' Before you know it you'll be drinking Pimms and opening the batting in a game of cricket.

Design . . . The Middle Class home shouldn't be all inherited antiques and Farrow & Ball; you need a few newer things too, things that have been Designed. Ideally those big, comfy armchairs with the little footrest that emerges when you lean back would be Middle Class, but sadly, they are not. Instead, there are a lot of rather uncomfortable chairs and articulated lights available. If your guests or wife start complaining of bad backs and sore eyes, tell them the name of the Designer and they'll be so impressed they will quite forget their distress.

It *can't* be the chair darling, it's a Phillipe Shark design

Rescue Remedy

Donkey Sanctuaries . . . Sometimes in Middle Class dynasties the head of the family becomes disillusioned with the other family members, convinced that they are toadying up to them because they want to inherit the house in the Dordogne or The True Sword of Genghis Khan. In these circumstances it is not unusual for the head honcho to bypass the family and bequeath the lot to the local Donkey Sanctuary. This explains why you see so many donkeys living in Sandbanks and driving around in Jaguars

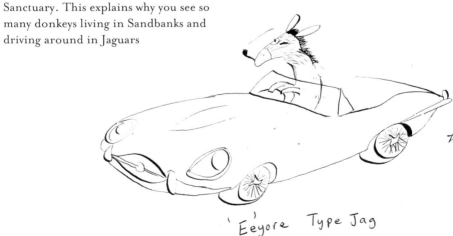

'Eeyore' Type Jag

Daylesford Farm Shop . . . Shortly before the French Revolution Marie Antoinette had a play-farm in the grounds of her château, Le Petit Trianon. It was free of mud and was stocked with freshly washed and perfumed lambs for her to cuddle. In the twenty-first century Poshwolds there is the Daylesford 'Farm Shop' (to this day no one has ever seen a real farmer in there). Everything wooden has been painted French Grey, including all the trees in the ~~car~~ 4x4 park. The vegetables are displayed most decoratively in enormous baskets and look as though their destiny lies more as an extra in a period drama than in soup. Cynics ask: should a Farm Shop be allowed to call itself such when it has its own spa?

Typical farmer (circa 1960)

Downton Abbey . . . Most people watch *Upstairs Downstairs Abbey* to criticise what's wrong with it. But watch we do, by the millions. Not since *Brideshead Revisited* have Middlings all sat down to watch the same thing at the same time. Despite the inevitable historical inaccuracies, I'm looking forward to next week's episode, which will be dealing with the suspenseful period around the outbreak of the Falklands War, when Edward VIII abdicated, women got the vote and man bounced on the moon.

Diesel . . . Or Rudolf Diesel, to give it its full name (this is actually true), is the fuel of choice for powering the 4x4s and estate cars that transport the Middle Classes around the country. It is a point of constant irritation for Diesel-car-owning Middlings that in Britain Diesel is more expensive than petrol and yet on the Continent it is considerably cheaper: *another* good reason to emigrate. One way of getting our money's worth is helping ourselves to lots of the free gloves that are supplied next to the pumps, having, as they do, many uses in the home and garden, such as polishing the silver, pruning the bunting and, particularly, cheese-making.

Daily Mail . . . This Royal Family fanzine is sneered at by everyone in public and yet in private we are devouring it, as it is one of the only papers with a healthy circulation. It is mainly read by women, and the few men who buy it pretend it's for the extensive sports coverage and the Fred Basset cartoon, which has been running for 50 years (350 in dog years) and is ~~yet to make anyone laugh~~ consistently hilarious.

Dolphins . . . The opportunity to swim with Dolphins is often cited by Middlings as being one of the things you simply must do before you die. No one has ever asked the Dolphins what *they* think, just assuming that they would be honoured to rub shoulders (flippers) with a landscape architect from Hebden Bridge. They actually find it incredibly annoying, and across the planet have struck deals with sharks to job share. As a consequence, it is becoming less popular.

Date Nights . . . There comes a time in every Middle Class couple's life when we have told each other all our stories, are too tired for any intimacy and the only thing we have left in common is the children. To punish ourselves for this impasse we go out on Date Nights. The object of these nights is to try and talk about anything other than the children for as long as possible. The winner is the one who manages to stay awake beyond the starter.

Deck Shoes . . . Most Middlings possess a pair of these. The groovework in the soles is ideal for the harsh, wet, slippery and salty conditions we encounter on the decking outside gastropubs throughout the summer months. Worn without socks by all ages and sexes, the popularity of the Deck Shoe has led to some cases of very Middle Class children from around Aldeborough and the North Norfolk Coast being born with them instead of feet.

Dishwashers . . . Middle Class dishwasher etiquette is almost as much of a minefield as the compost. Woe betide the helpful guest who just stacks it and turns it on. In some households everything has to be rinsed (thoroughly washed) by hand before being put in the machine, in others it's, 'Nothing wooden' or, 'Don't put the knives in with the pointy bit poking up, do you want someone to fall on that and be stabbed to death?' What is the chance of that actually happening? The head of the household normally completely restacks it after everyone has gone to bed anyway. Secretly, everyone knows it would be far quicker to do it all by hand, and the nostalgical Middling may even remember the time when the whole family gathered round the sink after lunch and sang as they either dried up or put away.

Designated Driver . . . Since the police have proved that when we are drunk we are not actually driving as brilliantly as we think we are, Middlings who want to enjoy anything more than a small sherry on their night out have to decide who's going to drive home afterwards. If you are unlucky enough to be singled out for this role, the normal course of action is to knock back as much booze as you possibly can the moment you arrive at the pub or party. Having fallen over a few times and said 'Slorry' quite loudly, someone more responsible will fill your shoes. Hopefully the hangover you receive the following morning will be considered punishment enough.

Digging Down . . . Middlings love to expand, and once the attic has been converted into the au pair's bedroom, we've removed all the downstairs walls and have built a conservatory, the only way left to go is down. Not surprisingly given how damp things are underground with water tables and whatforth, what starts out as a cinema, snug and gym suite soon becomes a wet room, then indoor pond, before eventually the entire house falls down.

Delicatessens . . . There are few places where a Middling with a rumbling tummy would rather find themselves than a Deli. For starters, they are always run by fellow Middlings, which instantly puts us at ease; for main course, they are stuffed with products made by friends, or friends of friends; and for pudding, they are *not* supermarkets, so there is a worthy feel-good factor about shopping there as well. On the downside they are always too small and everything you buy tastes of cheese.

Deli Belly

E is for Elephant Orphanages...

Elderflower . . . In the last few years Middlings have been completely rolled over by Elderflower Power. Everything we could possibly want is now available in Elderflower flavour: cordial, sorbet, Prosecco, candles, even mattress toppers (this last one is clearly nonsense, in case anyone is interested). One of the finest sights in spring is a flock of Middlings wearing Crocs and filling baskets with plump white elderflower heads. It should, of course, really be called *younger*flower, as the elderly flowers actually smell like tomcat spray.

Echinacea . . . You need only reach for a hanky or Handy Andy (if they still exist) in a Middle Class household and the Echinacea tablets are whipped out and forced down your throat. In a real emergency, like a cricked neck or a broken leg, they are not as effective as the mighty Rescue Remedy, but they are not to be sniffed at (you swallow them). For maximum effect, wash them down with a glass of scotch, a spoonful of honey and a mug of Lemsip, just to be on the safe side.

Ecomentalism . . . Properly poor people can't afford to worry about the environment and the absurdly rich are absurdly rich *because* they don't worry about the environment, which rather leaves it up to us Middlings to SAVE THE WORLD. We do *try* and do our bit by eating leftovers, watching documentaries about polar bears and driving diesel cars, but deep down we know it's not really enough. We realise that if we truly want to save the planet we should stop having children, strap windmills to our chimney pots, use our bicycles, stop flying to Puglia and not have a ten-minute power shower every morning. But then we wouldn't feel like Middlings any more, which would be even worse than no world.

Eggshell Paint . . . Not the charming ritual of painting on eggshells with children at Easter time, for which any paint (or felt-tip pen) may be used, but rather the great tins of Farrow & Ball Eggshell we use to paint the woodwork in the house. The Middle Class finish of choice used to be the rather flashy full gloss, which is actually more practical, having a shiny, wipeable surface. Perhaps the real reason Middlings so love the Eggshell finish is because its dullness mirrors ours?

Eton Mess . . . Before he went up to Oxford, when Pippin and Snipe's great-grandfather was still at Eton, he was shooting a grouse from his balcony, which startled Cook, who dropped the pavlova and in that moment Eton Mess was born. It has been a great relief to clumsy Middle Class pavlova makers ever since. Any soft fruit can be combined with broken meringue and whipped cream to create what is unquestionably one of the world's finest puddings. For a truly authentic version, add some blood, feathers and bone fragments from the Red Grouse (*Lagopus lagopus scoticus*, available from good game dealers, highly seasonal).

Eating Outside . . . It is a tribute to the formative years spent shivering on rugby and netball fields that Middlings are able to defy the elements and dine *al fresco* all summer long. It is our way of saying 'anything you can do we can do too' to those Middlings who have ~~static caravans~~ farmhouses in Italy. The terraces of Puglia, ~~smug~~ snug with shady vines and wafted over by the scents of rosemary and lavender, are *absolutely no better* than a back garden in Cumbria, with its mildewy bunting strung between a couple of *leylandiis,* and a slight whiff of gas from next door's patio heater.

Entertainers at Children's Parties . . . Sadly, the best children's entertainers are on the Paedophile Register and are no longer allowed within 50m of children, which means their performances lack intimacy. Parents should really agree amongst themselves to keep things cheap and cheerful, with basic games based around the simple premise of suddenly stopping the music. The problem begins with one parent raising the bar and taking the whole of Buttercup's class by LearJet to Lapland to meet Santa Christmas, staying in a suite at the Ice Hotel and giving party bags that contain lifetime passes to Disney World. Pass the parcel, even with a genuine barely used Rubik's Cube as the main prize, doesn't quite cut the mustard after that.

Elgar . . . Synonymous with notes of a musical and monetary (£20) variety, Elgar is also a Middle Class pin-up of *note*. His Nimrods, in various forms, can cause even the stiffest of British upper lips to tremble. The tragedy for Elgar was that he *was* a Middling, and apparently he rather wished he wasn't. The annual inclusion of his smash hit 'Land of Hope and Glory' at the Last Night of the Proms has (annoyingly for him) put him at the very heart of Middle Class Britain for evermore.

Egyptian Cotton . . . Gradually Middlings have cottoned on to the beauty of quality cotton. In the old days, when pyjamas had buttons, everything was made of cotton, but then someone invented polyester, which was ~~modern~~ horrible. We compromised and had poly/cotton for a bit, this dried quickly but was still quite sweaty, so we went back to pure cotton, got bored again and have finally discovered there is a ~~pedigree chum~~ premier cru of cotton, Egyptian Cotton. No one actually knows what's so special about it but if it was good enough for the Mummies it's good enough for the Yummy Mummies!

Yummy Mummies

Eating at Table . . . There is a huge gulf between how Middle Class families *actually* behave and how we would *like* them to. It is a cause of deep disappointment that Eating at Table is now something that has to be forced on unwilling family members. We look longingly across the Channel to Italy, where ten generations of the same family sit huggero-muggero around a table groaning with seasonal produce, talking over each other, laughing and gesticulating, and we wonder where we've gone wrong. In the old days, Archipelago and Mufty could be bribed with the threat of no pudding if they didn't sit tight till the bitter end, but now the promise of blackberry and apple crumble just sounds like a nightmare of broken phones to them.

Ethnic . . . Due in part to Middlings' liberal world-view, happy memories from the gap year and competitive pricing, Ethnic goods are extremely prevalent in Middle Class homes. Everything from coffee tables, mirrors, beds and poofs to shrunken heads and pot-pourri bowls are available in Ethnic. But the king of Ethnic nick-nacks are salad spoons. Almost every Middle Class household has, in a drawer, a slightly sticky salad spoon and fork carved in endangered wood topped off with African safari mammals, and very ethnice they are too.

Emma Bridgewater . . . As Oscar Fry once tweeted wittily, 'The Middle Classes get the crockery they deserve' (someone should check this, it doesn't seem very witty to us). We can only thank our Emma Bridgewater navy stars that we live in the age we do. From colourful spots (which is clearly where Damien Hirst got his idea from) to fun foodie words like EGGS and the educational bird series, Emma Bridgewater crockery is as contagious as Foot & Mouth. Being thick and chunky in shape, it is not only satisfying on the eye but it also gives the pieces a sporting chance when being prewashed in the Belfast Sink or thrown in jest at the man of the house when he has forgotten to take the recycling bins out for the second week in a row (I *had* said I was sorry).

is for Facepainting...

Festivals . . . Festivals are no longer about fruity fun, free love, LSD and the Grateful Dead; they are now as much a part of the Middle Class year as a week in Cornwall with an organic veg box. The greatest fun is had by the children, who run about in relative safety spending their parents' money and staying up all night while the aforementioned parents are too high on magic mushroom bhajis to care, for once. Despite the fact that we are camping on a mudslide and have to walk everywhere, Festivals have become rather expensive. It costs the same for a Middling to rent a villa in Umbria for a week as it does to take Geronimo, Cosima and Pluto to a festival. The longest queue is not for the self composting latrines but for the cashpoint machine.

4x4s . . . As much as Middlings love to drive 4x4s they are wracked with guilt by it. Those who buy them have very good reasons: some say it is because they live in town and everyone's got one; others say it is for safety; a few mumble about snow, or the dog, or Emmenthal's cello. We can see why the Americans all drive them – they are a very big-boned nation and would not fit into ordinary cars – but we are a lither people and yet our Isles are sinking under the weight of these enormous vehicles. You can be sure that the parking places painted on to the tarmac outside Lidl are considerably narrower than those outside Waitrose (we've never been to a Lidl, but think this might be true). And the cost of the fuel that they use taking Measles, Mumps and Rubella to and from school is now as much as their school fees (but not if you include the extras).

Foodies . . . It is becoming increasingly difficult to find Middlings who aren't Foodies. Since smoking was banned and cars became too complicated to work on, cooking and eating have become the Middle Class hobby of choice. To qualify as a Foodie you have to be genuinely upset when you run out of Pink Himalayan Salt; make your own bread, vinegar or jam; have an enormous collection of cookery books, some of which you've actually cooked things from; go to Farmers' Markets; and know what samphire is. Beware of False Foodies; they are greedy people who eat all day long under the cover of it being their hobby.

France . . . France is not a real place, it is a paradise invented by Middlings where everything is perfect. The roads are free from traffic, the food is exquisite, the women beautiful and often bare-chested, the men are generous lovers, you shop in markets where wee-stained peasants in floral housecoats man stalls that burst forth with local, seasonal fare. The weather is better than ours, as is the education system. House prices are lower, the health service more healthy and less queuey, the wine cheaper and the cheeses have recognisable names and are made by real cheese-makers. There are only two snags: the first is the French themselves, which we have addressed, and our programme of replacing them with British Middlings is almost complete. The second is Rabies, but even heaven needs some jeopardy.

Fly Fishing . . . Only Middle Class men could have taken something that was already quite hard to do then make it considerably harder, on purpose. The Fly Fisherman will almost never catch a fish but will spend hour after happy hour away from home, in a costume of tweed and corduroy, fiddling with his flies, detangling his line or removing his hook from passing badgers caught by his back cast. If you *do* love your wife and fancy a bit of trout for your supper but don't live anywhere near a supermarket or trout farm, then forget about flies, put a large piece of cake on the end of a hook and dangle it in some water. You will almost certainly catch something, and in the unlikely event that you don't, you can at least eat your bait on the way home.

Foraging . . . It's ironic that although Middlings have never before had so much incredible food available in Waitroses all over the land 24 hours a seven, we should chose this moment in history to put on our wellies, go into the woods with a basket and try and pick free stuff. Country Middlings have always dabbled in a little light Foraging – blackberries, mushrooms, sloes and soforth – but it didn't used to be called Foraging; it was called going for a walk with a bag in your pocket. In the last few years, it has been rebranded and is now a must-do Middle Class lifestyle choice, with bramble-proof knee gaiters, hats with mushroom pockets and truffle-spotting apps for the cleverphone. It's a particular nightmare for murderers, who used to have the woods to themselves for burying their victims and who now have to explain their business to a family of trowel-wielding Middlings from Islington.

Corpse

Farrow & Ball . . . Sounding like an important innovation from the agricultural revolution, Farrow & Ball has been a huge hit with the Middle Classes. All their colours are different shades of grey, apart from French Grey, which is green. They are made the traditional way by bare-footed peasant children, using mud, blood and clay (this isn't true, we don't want to get sued, they are actually made by factory workers wearing protective clothing). Few Middlings can afford to buy whole tins of the paint, but show their enthusiasm for it by applying dabs from tester pots all over the house, normally near light switches for maximum noticeability. Parsimonious Middlings are very keen on getting their local paint shop to mix up pots of their cheaper own-brand paint to match the Farrow & Ball colours. This is a laughable deceit, which, rather like using rock salt as opposed to Maldon, a good Middling can spot a mile off.

Fun . . . The more a Middling assures you something will be Fun, the more you know that it probably won't. 'Let's walk the seven peaks!' 'But it's snowing!' 'Come on, it'll be Fun!' It wasn't and it cost the taxpayer a fortune in air ambulances. Fun is our rallying cry, and if it has bunting around it, it's even *more* Fun. 'Look at my new hat, I thought it was rather Fun!' 'Oh yes! What Fun!' (What you're both actually saying is that it's simply ghastly.)

Farmers' Markets . . . Before the advent of the Farmers' Market, Middlings had given up on regular markets, which were only any good if you wanted family packets of out-of-date chicken wings, beach towels with tigers on them or fluffy slippers. Suddenly we can buy vegetables covered in mud, cheeses made by pop stars, smoked trout pâté and freshly squeezed apple juice, and best of all, there aren't any (real) grumpy farmers within a million miles of a Farmers' Market and the stalls are all run by our friends. It's almost like being in France but without the constant threat of rabies hanging over everything.

Normal Market £1   Farmers Market £1

Fireworks . . . Like barbeques and chicken legs, Fireworks are entirely the domain of Middling males. It's the bigger the better with Fireworks. Garden Fireworks are fine for indoors, but in the garden you need the enormous and fabulously expensive display ones. Middling women do the oohing when the explosions are beautiful and the children do the aahing when they grab the wrong end of a sparkler and set fire to their cashmere mittens. We grown-ups enjoy sparklers, too, as we furiously sign our names in the air while quietly sighing about the demise of cheques. Watching Fireworks to the accompaniment of famous passages of classical music is popular amongst Vintage Middlings, but it doesn't carry the same danger factor as bonfire night and almost never involves toffee apples or the Fire Brigade.

Fêtes . . . Fêtes used to be quite bloodthirsty events, with bare-knuckle boxing, shin-kicking and wife-selling on the programme. These days Middlings have taken them over and they are a bit more family-friendly. For adolescent males there is still some violence with 'Splat the Rat' and the Coconut Shies. For grown-ups there is ~~the buzzing wire game~~ a beer tent. Students can enjoy the whole thing ironically; there's always heaps of bunting and it's a great opportunity to wear fun wellies. We just feel so sorry for Jean-Paul Sartre, who can't enjoy them at all.

Colin Firth . . . Despite his not very Middle Class first name, Colin Firth has been taken to Middling hearts. If we had to vote for our monarchy, there is a very good chance he would be crowned King Colin the Firtht.

Fancy Dress . . . Middlings love fancy-dress parties because they are double fun, just like the expression 'wood warms you twice' (once when you stack it up, then again when it falls down and you have to restack it but better). You have a heap of fun choosing your costume, then all the fun of the party.

One of the strange things about Fancy Dress is its ability to disappear over the course of the night. By the end hardly anyone is still wearing it. Where does it go? *We're* still in our chicken suit . . .

Hey
come back!
We were going
to share a
taxi

Flower Arranging . . . As long as flowers grow there will be Middlings to arrange them. Some lucky Middlings are born Flower Arrangers, others go on expensive courses where they learn the complicated art of putting flowers in a vase *or* jug *stalk* first and not forgetting the *water*.

It is telling that the most famous Middle Class Flower Arranger of all time, Constance Spry, is better known for inventing Coronation Chicken – where she found the time we have NO idea.

Farm Shops . . . For the Middle Classes, shopping in a Farm Shop tends to be a weekend treat. The secret of enjoying a Farm Shop is not to break the spell, so don't ask too many questions. We like to think that all the produce has come from the actual farm we are shopping in, or at least a neighbouring one. Unfortunately, the truth of the matter is that they are generally little more than shops in farms and at least 50% of the crop will have come from Peru.

Fish . . . There is something very Middle Class about Fish. What with the swimming and schooling and baskets and whatforth. The first thing we always think about when it comes to Fish is ~~chips~~ sustainability. We all know that there are hardly any left in the sea, that, insanely, fisherman are only allowed to catch about three Fish a year, and after that they can go out and kill them for fun but aren't allowed to eat or sell them. Middlings are resigned to eating only Fish that they have caught themselves (highly unlikely: *see* Fly Fishing), have been bashed on the head with a pole and garrotted with a line (expensive), or that have jumped out of little Jupiter's goldfish bowl in the night (heartless).

Fish Fingers (for adults) . . . There is an increasing reluctance amongst Middlings to grow up, and nowhere is this more evident than in our eating habits. Sweets (apart, of course, from those travel ones found stuck together in round tins in the glove box), ice cream and Fish Fingers were once only the victuals of children. Times change, and these days Fish Fingers are served with a dollop of homemade tartare sauce and a dash of irony to grown-ups in houses and gastropubs up and down the land. Those Middlings who feel ashamed by their paedofishy tendencies, pop the bread-crumbed fish sticks between slices of bread and call them Fish Finger Sandwiches. The twang of guilt really hits home when you behold a school of eight Fish Fingers spanning your plate and remember that Strudella and Puissance eat only two.

Fairtrade . . . One of the most noble traits that Middlings exhibit is a willingness to engage our consciences when shopping. Clearly the most important consideration when buying something is ~~the price~~ the working conditions and wages of the producer. All sorts of very useful products are available with the Fairtrade classification, including coffee, chocolate and those tubes filled with seeds that when you turn them on their heads make a sound like rain. You know you are on safe Middle Class territory when you enter a 'Fairtrade Town'. It's so heart-warming to know that the stream of coins you pop into the 'no change given' pay-and display machine in the town centre will be going to the families of the gypsies who tarmacced the car park, and not some greedy council whose prohibitive charges have forced most shoppers to abandon the town in favour of the retail village on the ring road, where they can park for free.

French Junk . . . Someone else's junk is always more interesting than our own, which is why Middlings go *Ooh la la* for old French tat. Particularly popular are bashed-up pieces of enamel, jugs and containers, preferably with some French writing on them, which puts their ~~Provence~~ provenance beyond doubt. Sadly, the French don't like our rubbish in the same way, so we can't swap Grandma's nest of reproduction mahogany occasional tables for a sign with the Michelin man on it, no matter how hard we try.

Fantasy Dinner Parties . . . It is a favourite Middle Class distraction while clearing up after a particularly boring dinner party to fantasise about who your ideal guests would be. It is considered obligatory to invite Peter Ustinov (though no one can quite remember who he is). Other guests normally include: Princess Diana, Nelson Mandela, Churchill, Gandhi, Jesus and someone from *Gardener's World* to offer advice about pruning the fig tree. Don't be complacent, though, just because it's a fantasy, it's amazing what can go wrong.

G is for Garden Centres...

Gastropubs . . . When it became impossible to leave a pub without a glass sticking out of our faces or a pool cue wrapped about our necks, Middlings decided it was time to invent the Gastropub. Up and down the land dartboards were replaced by stuffed badgers, horse brasses by enamel French signs and the bowls of ~~peanuts~~ peenuts lovingly marinated in forty different varieties of urine, by Greek olives. Eating has replaced drinking as the main activity, and where once chips were served with everything, now it is beetroot and goat's cheese. It's not all good news, however, the more we eat, the harder it becomes to squeeze between the tables, with inevitable results . . .

Gastropub fight

Gilding . . . Or the ~~Midas~~ Middle Class touch. You would expect most of Britain to be covered in gold when you consider how many Middlings have done Gilding courses. Quite what they do with the skill when they've mastered it is a mystery. You never see gold-plated husbands or 24-carat carrot cake. We would go so far as to suggest that if all the unused gold leaf in all the Middle Class cupboards were pooled, there would almost be enough to gild an entire American-style fridge.

Gardens . . . While Porcini and Greenfinch are small, the Garden is given over entirely to them and they generally use it to store their fun-coloured plastic slides, toys, trampolines and whatforth. Once they've left home, it acts as a kind of replacement therapy. We inflict our urge to nurture on the Garden, and quite quickly its well-being consumes us. Green-fingered Middlings are rightly very proud of their Gardens and will always drag the man who's come to read the meter around every tree, pond, wind-chime and shrubbery before they let him into the house. They do, of course, require constant attention, and can't possibly be left unsupervised for much more than an hour or two a day. Holidays are simply out of the question.

Gardeners . . . Most Middlings will at some time or other in their life reach the stage where they simply have to have a Gardener. One of the greatest joys in employing a Gardener is having something new to complain about. You do rather get what you pay for with them, but try and avoid the *very* expensive ones, who are as Middle Class as you are, or you'll find yourself wasting hours making them coffee in the cafetière and working out which people you know in common.

Grandparents . . . *See* Free Childcare.

Green & Black's . . . Named after the two colours that Wellington boots used to be available in, Green & Black's is a heavyweight Middle Class chocolate brand with serious ~~ganache~~ panache.

Growing Your Own . . . It is all the rage for Middlings to spend hours and hours and hundreds of pounds Growing Our Own vegetables, and since the invention of grow-bags, the excuse of not having a garden no longer holds any sway. There is a brief, five minute window when our home-grown baby broad beans are quite delicious, but while our back is turned (removing the blackfly from the peas) they will have grown enormous, chewy and grey. The same can be said for courgettes, which seem hell-bent on defying the modest photograph on the seed packet by becoming marrows, bigger even than the peach young James escaped from his wicked aunts in. If you are thinking of selling your surplus crop, then it would be worth considering growing marijuana, which can have an enormous street value.

Gap Years . . . Once the ghastly business of paying for Talisker and Panda's education is over, there is one final turn of the wringer for the Middle Class parent to endure, the Gap Year. It is great fun for the young, as they get to cram in their lifetime's quota of risk-taking, danger and unpasteurised milk into a mere six months (it's rarely a full year, as they spend the first six months 'raising money' to pay for the trip, which they completely fail to do as they are always in bed, which annoys the parents so much they cave in and pay for it all themselves). It doesn't really matter where they go, as long as it's somewhere where you simply mustn't drink the tap water. On their return, don't go and meet them at the airport, for covered in tattoos, pierced as Brosnans, shoeless, with matted hair and clutching enormous drums, you will not be able to recognise them.

Grand Designs . . . Increasingly, Middlings are realising that once their chicks have flown the nest it's time to knock down the family house and build something much, much bigger. The television show *Grand Designs* is the inspiration behind this phenomenon, and Middlings across the land are glued to it, no matter how many times it's repeated. 'Ooh, this is the bit when they deliver the expensive glass from Germany and the crane nearly falls over. I love the look on Kevin's face!' Whether they start with a mock-Tudor lighthouse or an outside lavatory, they always end up creating what looks like a visitor centre, with very ~~uncomfortable~~ modern kitchen chairs.

Gingham . . . Gingham is the default Middle Class pattern of choice. It is unquestionably good taste. The men favour it for shirts, while the womenfolk find uses for it not only in their wardrobe but throughout the house. It makes pretty curtains, excellent bath hats for jam, and when we dream of France, the bistro table will be spread with a red gingham cloth. The only place we don't like to see it is on drying-up cloths. Gingham drying-up cloths tend to be the cheap ones you find in pound shops and don't even have the benefit of being fun, such as those that sport Labradors or define rugby as 'a game played by men with odd-shaped balls'.

Godparents and Godchildren . . . Being a Godparent means providing one thing: ~~spiritual wellbeing~~ presents. Sticklers for tradition have small services in churches (empty old buildings with leaky roofs), but it is quite normal amongst Middlings to be simply rung up and given the glad tidings that you have been picked as one of only twenty-five special people to be a Godparent for little Atilla. If you are a banker then be reassured that it is quite normal to be chosen, even if you only met the child's parents once, fleetingly, in the checkout at Waitrose.

Game Fair . . . Once a year all the animals that haven't been shot come together and have a fair to celebrate the fact. Country-based Middle Class humans turn up too, in their thousands, despite the animals moving it to a different location each year. They generously allow the eager Middlings to think they are helping out by walking around the show ring with them and also allow them to run stalls selling various things (mainly organic beer and horse polish). The slogan for the Game Fair is, famously, 'four legs good, 4x4s even better'.

Gurkhas . . . The sight of a Gurkha walking arm in arm with Joanna Lovely is one of the top ten Middle Class lifetime sightings. There is something about a Gurkha which makes us warm inside, like a curry. Don't ask a Gurkha to show you his knife, though; he's not allowed to resheath it until he has drawn blood, and it's surprising how much a cat can bleed.

Ghastly . . . Or in its fuller form, *Simply Ghastly*, is the Middle Class adjective of choice for expressing displeasure at something or more likely some*one* behind their back. It's a splendid word that you can really draw out, adding the bonus insult *'arse'* in the middle, for maximum effect.

Gourmet Burgers . . . In the same way Middlings use *gastro* pubs and *boutique* hotels, we now have *Gourmet* Burgers. This is just so you are quite sure that you will not be eating teeth, ground gristle and other unrecognisable bits of cow. Those traditional burgers are for children.

Grammar . . . Ever since Trynn Lust wrote his book about shooting pandas, Middling bonnets have been buzzing with concern over the nation's Grammar. We particularly seem to have it in for greengrocers and market stallholders, who cheerfully insert apostrophe's wherever they think one might jolly things up. This is silly. We all know what they mean by 'apple's' *and* we have the bonus of feeling clever for spotting that it's grammatically a mistake. So we say, 'Green Grocer's of Britain, ignore the proselytising and carry on apostrophising!'

Game . . . As in animals, which some Middlings enjoy killing and almost everyone (except vegetarianists) enjoys eating. The list of Game includes all sorts of things, such as pheasants, grouses, blackbirds, bluetits, great tits, nuthatches, goldfinches and robins (hmm, these sound suspiciously like garden birds, we might have got our lists muddled). There is, as you would hope, a lot of fun involved with Game. It starts with the getting hold of it, either by dint of your own skill (shooting) or fast driving (road kill). Then there is the skinning, plucking and drawing (removing of the guts with an HB pencil), which brings you uncomfortably close to the grim reality of death and in most cases drives you back to Waitrose.

Golf . . . This is a game that used to be played endlessly by Middle Class men. Much to their annoyance, in recent times women and sports personalities have taken it up too *and* have shown not a little aptitude. Oscar Fry wittily described it as 'a good walk ruined', but he has a club foot and is bedridden, so is not in a position to judge. We played it once but weren't very good, we kept potting the white ball and never even *saw* the coloured ones.

Glamping . . . Suffering, or camping, as it used to be known, has thankfully been entirely replaced by the much more glamorous (expensive) and comfortable Glamping. No more do Middlings have to struggle with guy ropes, rain, gas bottles or wee buckets. With Glamping it's all spacious teepees, yurts, bunting, kilims, shiny chrome Airstream caravans, gypsy wagons, bell tents, shepherds' huts, tree houses, bunting, hot showers, four-poster beds, sheepskin rugs, flushing lavatories (with wooden seats), wood-burning stoves, bunting and free-range eggs. A glamp-site does cost a bit more than a five-star hotel, but it's worth it, to really get back to nature.

Gift Shops . . . Young Middlings believe the only reason why galleries, museums and statelies exist is for the shopping opportunities they offer. One wonders what on earth Hercules and Crayfish could possibly want with Tudor scented candles or padded tapestry bed trays, but they and other children cram the gift shops to such an extent that it becomes impossible to turn around and flee the place without knocking something over. The crystal Wedgewood glitterdome smashes to pieces, of course, and we have to cough up for it. It's a good business plan and a far cry from the days of the glass tumbler filled with fringed leather bookmarks with line drawings of the castle in gold. What with the advent of eBooks, cleverphones and iThings, bookmarks are now the only souvenirs you will *not* find in a Gift Shop.

Glyndebourne . . . Although it is really one of the last Sebastions of the Properly Posh, Glyndebourne is still on the radar of picnic-loving Middlings. It is for many a lifetime's ambition realised, sheltering behind an ancient yew hedge in black tie, being beaten on the head by hail on an August evening, clinging on to the hamper and chairs while the chorizo and samphire tarts turn cartwheels across the perfect lawn. It's what ~~migraines~~ memories are made of . . .

 **is for Hammocks...**

Houses . . . We love our Houses almost as much as our Labradors. However, as we grow older we don't get bigger and bigger Labradors, but we do get bigger and bigger Houses. Whether we are expanding to accommodate more children or to display our burgeoning wealth depends on the Middling in question. The rest of Europe wonder why we are so obsessed with buying Houses. The answer to this is simple: we grew up playing Monopoly, so actually it's amazing so few of us end up owning large, red hotels.

House prices . . . The secret behind the ~~smugness~~ quiet confidence most Middlings exude is the enormous value of our house(s). It used to be considered bad form to talk about House Prices, but now it has become a form of Middle Class tourettes that almost everyone who owns a house seems to suffer from. If we are ever feeling a bit blue, the surest way to cheer ourselves up is to get an estate agent over to value our house. We all love to hear those wonderful lies.

Herbs . . . It's almost impossible to believe that twenty years ago Middlings were happily sprinkling dusty old Herbes de Provence from a ~~irritating~~ charming little hessian sacks all over our cooking and thinking we were rather sophisticated. We knew about Parsley, he was a lion, and Rosemary, who was someone's aunt, but the rest of them we'd never heard of. We are finally making up for lost thyme. We buy them in little growing pots from Waitrose, snip off what we need and scatter it about abundantly on everything from omelettes to ice cream, and in some cases in the bath. Then we plonk the remains on the windowsill, where it gets either over- or under-watered to death in less than a week.

Horses . . . It is very much a part of being Middle Class to be on speaking terms with horses. Indeed, some are so attached to their horses that they tow them around behind their cars everywhere they go. Others are just happy knowing which end to put the Polo in. Thankfully, come the Cheltenham Festival or the Grand National, all our dormant horse knowledge miraculously springs to life and we are able to speak with conviction about how we fancy Downstairs Louis' chances in the Queen Mother's ~~Gin~~ Cup or that the going looks a bit heavy for Big Dick in the Champion Venison Steaks.

Hog Roasts . . . 'A most undignified end for a Hog' *Oscar Fry*... But a joy to the eyes and snouts of all non-vegetarian, non-Jewish, non-Muslim Middlings. They are the essential centrepiece to any outdoor Middle Class party, as they serve as a replacement kitchen for shyer and colder guests to congregate around. They are also gaining in popularity as a cheaper option for wedding feasts, where the fun factor nearly makes up for the rather conspicuous cost-cutting.

Heritage Vegetables . . . It's all very well growing your own vegetables, but it's even more Middle Class to go one better, and one better than home-grown vegetables is home-grown *Heritage* Vegetables. Why plant industrially modified carrots which balloon to the size of a cucumber within days but taste of nothing more than the salty water in which they were boiled, when you can grow the exact same variety of carrot that Henry VIII was nibbling on while composing Greensleaves, or the one that Peter Rabbit was munching moments before Mr McGregor blew his tail off with a shotgun?

House of Bruar . . . This is where the great Middling clans gather every summer, each in their own traditional cashmere. Here they feast and drink, indulge in friendly squabbles over the last navy blue sleeveless cardigan in a medium and generally jostle for position within the clan. When all is spent, some journey north to their hunting grounds and others head south for the winter, their bags bulging with everything they will need — from smoked cashmere to gold-plated fudge — to see them through the hard months ahead.

Harry Potter . . . Middling parents have a lot to thank J.K. Rowling-in-it for. Harry Potter is a role model they can thoroughly approve of. What with his private education in a good, mixed boarding school, his love of sport and his interest in owls, he is Middle Class through and through. He has also, in the same way that the Famous Five did years before, got young Middlings excited about reading. And Reading needs all the help it can get; halfway between Slough and Oxford, it is a rather unloved sort of place with far too many industrial estates and worryingly few artisan traders.

History . . . It is easy to spot Middlings in historical settings; we are the ones poring over a guidebook, reading out the facts and dates pertaining to the building. There is, of course, one thing we love to know *even* more than the History of things, and that is the History of ourselves. We are always seeking confirmation that we were once grander than our present status suggests. And if we had an Earl Grey, Viscount Biscuit, or even an Honourable Discharge in the family, we don't half go on about it. In serious cases we will write their biography, pay to have it published, and give it to the rest of the family for Christmas.

Hot-Water Bottles . . . Sadly, fewer and fewer people use 'hotties' these days. This is a shame, as they smell so good being filled, and do a fantastic job of making tiny parts of your body very hot indeed. It is also very interesting to see where they end up in the morning. Sometimes you wake with your hotty still slightly warm and clutched to your breast like a just dead lover; at other times you force them from you in the night and come morning discover them cold, limp and lifeless on the floor. Some people spoil their hotties, dressing them in expensive winter clothing; beautiful little *faux* fur jackets or cable-knit cashmere, far better than the clothes worn by their own children. Finally, what little boy doesn't glow with excitement when his grandmother tells him about the hotty waiting upstairs in bed for him.

Hummus . . . Who would have thought, when it arrived from the East (End) in the 1980s, stinking and pasty-faced, that hummus would replace chipolata sausages and chicken drumsticks as the children's party food of choice (the parents' choice) in 21st century Middle Class Britain? At Puffin's 5th birthday party you could hardly hear yourself think, 'I wish I had managed to book Siegfried and Roy, their tiger act would have ~~scared the shit out of~~ enchanted the little angels,' for the crunching of carrots and celery sticks smeared with the healthy spread.

Hoodies . . . What? You probably think Hoodies are not very Middle Class at all. Well here's the reassuring thing, some of them actually *are*. The signs are there for the observant to observe: if the hooded garments are either hand-knitted or made from cashmere, they're Middle Class. If the attack dog in whose company they are loitering is not a pit bull /staffie cross but a labrador puppy, they're Middle Class. And if on closer inspection their flick knives turn out to be Swiss army penknives with all the bits and bobs, or Opinels bought on the family holiday to Provence, they are beyond question, Middle Class.

Holidays . . . Middlings take Holidays very seriously and many of us become teachers just so we can have longer ones. We need at least three a year, a cold one (snowballing in the Alps or the Dolomites), a hot one (sunbathing in Puglia or Umbria) and a British one (sheltering in Cornwall or the Falklands).

 is for Invitations on the Mantlepiece...

Ivy . . . Middlings have mixed feelings about this bottle-green waxy climber. Most are convinced that it is trying to pull their houses down. The truth is that it is actually the Ivy which is holding the house up, and it is the process of pulling it off that causes the old place to disintegrate. Foolhardy Middlings declare an amnesty at Christmas and merrily snip off bits of Ivy to lie along the tops of picture frames and as decoration for the dinner table, unaware that, like eels, ivy is impossible to kill. It will try and burrow its way out through the walls from the inside, which does cause massive damage.

iThings . . . The enthusiasm Middlings have shown for gadgetries with i in front of them is quite impressive. It possibly has something to do with the iWatering (!) prices and iCatching (!!) yet simple designs. It can lead to confusion and heartbreak, though. We know of someone's son who wrote to Santa Christmas asking for an iCycle, which is a sort of bicycle. You can probably guess what happened, and not surprisingly the child has asked to be put up for adoption . . .

India . . . Thanks to ~~history~~. . . ~~cricket~~ . . . movies, India is a place that we Middlings hold affectionately in our hearts. Few are brave enough to actually visit it on account of the litter and the drains (lack of). However, we are very happy to eat their food and enjoy their ethnic style, both of which we consider great fun. Our favourite Indians are Ghandi, who we like so much we gave him an Oscar, and Mr Kipling, whose poetry keeps our peckers up and whose cakes keep our weight up. Following the success of naming so many British dogs after the famous Indian yoghurty drink, our affection for India has reached such a pitch that we are now paying the ultimate Middle Class compliment, the naming of our precious offspring after it.

Iced Coffee . . . This perennially popular Middle Class summer beverage (we know it isn't really, but we couldn't think of that many Is) is about as Middle Class as things get! The primary ingredient is Camp Coffee, which is only available from tiny village shops in the country. The Camp Coffee bottle strikes a considerable chord with Middlings, as it boasts on the label, not only a Gurkha and a Scotsman, each in national dress, but also a bell tent. There are moves afoot to re-name it Glamp Coffee.

Ice Cream . . . The abundance of rich, creamy and delicious Ice Cream found in today's Middle Class freezers is enough to make you want to be a spoon. Before we got our act together, Ice Cream came in three ~~flavours~~ colours – pink, brown and yellow – and was 90% pig fat. Its main use was as a bribe to encourage Peter and Jane to finish their mince and potatoes. Today's Pippit and Juniper are presented with flavours and textures that would make Willy Wonka weep. But not in our house. Modern Ice Creams are so good that we jealously guard them from any children that have ~~fallen down the chimney~~ come to visit. They don't appreciate the subtle brilliance of bitter chocolate sorbet or pistachio and amaretto crunch. For them, we stick lard, milk and yellow food colouring in the ice-cream maker . . . If it was good enough for us . . .

Inherited Things . . . There is nothing like the prospect of your sibling getting their hands on the Sheraton sideboard or Chipperfield magazine rack for it to suddenly be transformed from a brown and inconvenient waste of space into the most exquisite piece of furniture ever crafted. Middle Class eyes glow a very bright and unnatural green when a family member dies, and most feuds can be traced back either to board games or disputes over the division of the spoils. One side-effect of this being that any hard-won heirlooms are endowed with a supernatural mystique, quite to the bewilderment of visiting friends.

IKEA . . . For those corners of the Middle Class house which have escaped Aunt Florence's hand-me-downs there is IKEA. There is something instantly chic about a Scandinavian design outlet that you simply wouldn't get from a British shop selling similar things but called PineLand 'where everything is cheap as chipboard!'. The Swedes are exploiting the fact that few Middlings have actually been to Scandinavia so imagine it as a place of unbelievable stylishness. In reality it looks like rather like Croydon at night, but without the trams. It is also easy to get lost within the vastness of an IKEA. We have several friends who gave up trying to find their way out and now actually live there.

Isambard Kingdom Brunel . . . This brilliant top-hatted irongineer is very much a Middle Class pin-up. What with his trains, ships, bridges, channel chunnels and whatforth, no one has done more to help us travel about the kingdom than he. So much that we take for granted was invented by him; from the iPhone (the i stands for Isambard) to Irn-Bru (the Bru is short for Brunel). There is even a charming West Country tradition whereby once a week a very depressed Bristolian jumps off I.K.B.'s most famous creation, The Clifton Suspension Bridge, as a tribute to the great man.

Internet Shopping . . . As long as you are prepared to spend every moment of your life at home in readiness to receive your parcels, Internet Shopping is a wonderful development. It is surprising how quickly even Vintage Middlings have got the hang of it, when you consider how fiddlesome it is and how many opportunities there are to make mistakes . . .

Imperial System . . . It is fair to say that Middlings aren't all that keen on change. One of the most striking examples of this is our perseverance with the Imperial System. The very name causes our chests to swell, it's as proud and British as Armitage Shanks. The almost total incomprehensibility of it as a system is part of its charm, as is the fact that the rest of Europe don't want us to use it. You can always spot a Middling in a DIY shop by their insistence in asking for things in yards and extraordinarily small fractions of inches rather loudly.

Ice With Things In . . . Another example of how Middlings manage to improve on perfection. Just when we were starting to take ice for granted (most Middlings have American-style fridges which spew the stuff forth morning, noon and night) someone had the idea to freeze flowers and herbs within the cubes. Great fun in summer drinks, and Pimms in particular. A useful tip if you are having a Middle Class drinks party that you don't want to last too long, is to freeze stinging nettle leaves in your ice. That way your guests will just have one drink and then they'll leave pretty smartish when the ice melts and their lips and noses start getting unpleasantly stung . . .

Italy . . . Home to Tuscany, Umbria and Puglia, rather like France but further away so you can't really drive there with an aerodynamic plastic box strapped to the roof of your car. Italy is a place that makes Middlings sigh. We sigh at their art, their historical ruins, their beautiful people, their gardens, their food, their sports cars, their organised crime, their bunga bunga parties . . . The only things we enjoy finding fault with are the way that they govern and the terrifying way they drive. But we're the ones with ~~egg~~ Cornetto on our faces; it turned out recently that most of *our* politicians were on the fiddle too, and not even Jeremiah Clarkson, the patron saint of Middling motorists, can get beyond second gear on most British roads due to traffic jams, speed cameras and too many confusing signs.

J is for John Lewis...

Jam . . . From the base of the noble Bakewell Tart to the bleeding core of the humble doughnut, and the blob which slides down the clotted cream on the disputably pronounced scone, to the scarlet seam that runs through the Queenly victoria sponge, there is Jam. Cut a Middling open and it is Jam that will pour forth. (This is whimsy, it is, of course, blood, don't cut your thumb off if you've run out of Bonne Maman.) Despite the fact that there are really only two good flavours – red and orange – Middlings insist on experimenting with making it out of all sorts of inappropriate things like samphire, celeriac and even bunting, then stand over the bubbling pan like worried witches wondering why it's not setting but terrified to boil it for too much longer in case the flavour disappears.

Jersey Royals . . . Like the yearning that the mighty salmon feels, which pulls him back across oceans to the very river where he first was spawned, one morning in ~~Februay Febura~~ spring an inner voice speaks to all Middlings and whispers 'Jersey Royals'. We find they're never quite as good as the name suggests, but for the few republican-minded Middlings out there, these are their favourite Royals.

Jack Russells . . . The smallest of the Middle Class dogs and by far the most trouble. Most Middlings acquire a Jack Russell only to make their children look good by comparison. When not destroying the house, barking constantly or chasing the neighbours' cat, they are very Middle Class in their behaviour, loving, as they do, old music, country walks, food, open fires, cricket and digging down.

Jamie Oliver . . . Although he pretends in a tongue-in-cheeky-chappie way not to be Middle Class, we all know he is. And were you to chop up his name with a nice sharp knife, you would find that it contains no fewer than three Middle Class foodstuffs: jam, liver and ieo (the last one is definitely a Danish pâté), so his destiny as a chef was never in doubt. He is, in fact, *two* people. There's one called Jamie, who does all the clever cooking, and then there's a ~~patronising~~ altruistic one called Oliver, who tries to improve the nosh in the workhouse and then cries because everyone still wants pizza.

Please Sir, could I have a pizza?

John Betjeman . . . The only Poet Laureate that people have heard of and actually liked (unless you live in Slough). A Middling himself, he hovered about the fringes of the aristocracy observing in rhyme, talking about churches and generally making a charming nuisance of himself. When interviewed shortly before his death in his beloved Cornwall (he was the first outsider to discover the region, when hiding from the people of Slough, who had issued a fatwa), he said he wished he had ~~been to the orthodontist as a child~~ had more sex.

Jigsaw Puzzles . . . As Oscar Fry once asked wittily, 'Can anyone see a sky-coloured piece with some leaves on the prongy bit?' The answer to that was probably 'No', but Jigsaw Puzzles still do play an important part in Middle Class lives and often come out at Christmas as a device for escaping the arguments. They are one of those rare activities where age is no handicap, being four or eighty makes little difference to your puzzling abilities. Beware of Middle Class households which don't let you look at the picture on the box; they will probably not tell you which bed you are sleeping in either, which at the time can be annoying but can result in hilarious anecdotes to tell over the puzzle the next morning, while you're struggling to work out if it's Titian's *Rape of Europa* or the Arsenal team photo (less likely).

Jerusalem . . . Despite it being even further away than Cornwall, Jerusalem enjoys a strange hold over Middle Class schoolchildren. The hymn, written by William Blake, is the unofficial national anthem of England and the official school song for everywhere from Eton to Borstal. There is also a nobbly root vegetable called a Jerusalem artichoke which is spelled with a sometimes silent and other times quite noisy 'f'.

Jodhpurs . . . Designed by a dashing Indian polo player in the 1890s, these hard-to-spell, creamy-coloured trousers are the leggings of choice for all Middlings who think they may ever come into contact with a horse or know of someone who has. With the grippy calf section and baggier thigh part, they instantly give the wearer a swagger and a certain authority, particularly when used in conjunction with a large whip.

Jilly Cooper . . . The Jilly Cooper is the souped-up version of the standard Jilly. She corners better, has more horsepower and is far, far racier. For many adolescent female Middlings, she is the author of their first proper grown-up book and opens their eyes to the real world, a world ~~beyond the impossible romantic horsey dreams of childhood~~ of sex and horses.

Jars (storage) . . . Ever since Pooh put the remains of a balloon in a Jar and gave it to Eeyore as a birthday present, Middlings have had a great fondness for putting things in Jars. They appeal to our squirrelling instinct and aesthetic sensibilities at the same time. They look like chubby little penguins, all lined up with orange rubber beaks and tummies full of delicious things like stale walnut halves, very plain flour and some kind of sugar, which might be granulated or caster or actually probably salt.

Jane Austen . . . A prolific and popular writer of TV shows, films, books and eBooks, sadly dead now but when alive, Middle Class through and through. Strangely, as a Middling herself, her stories often involve marrying out of Middle Class into the Properly Posh, which isn't very sporting. To most female Middlings, she sets the benchmark in story-telling. Her subjects include Georgian vicarages, country walks, Bath and people saying clever things. She blew hot and cold with titles, though, from the rather boring *Emma* and *Mansfield Park* to the thrillingly alliterating *Pride and Prejudice*, *Sense and Sensibility* and *Dog and Dogging*.

K is for Kippers...

Kitchens . . . Apart from a fire on the floor, a goat in the corner and fleas in the wimple, modern Middlings now live exactly like our medieval predecessors – in the Kitchen. By knocking down every wall in sight, we are at least trying to make them big enough to accommodate all the Kitchen clobber. Every few years we rip out the cupboards and work surfaces replacing them with whatever is the latest must'ave. In the past month alone the fashion in work surfaces has gone from retro formica to wood, to granite, to zinc, to glass and now to polished nougat. But why do we bother? Once we've got our Kitchen just so, we completely cover it up; the work surfaces with breadmakers, espresso machines, Magimixes and blenders, and those beautiful cupboard doors with our children's ~~terrible scribbles~~ lovely paintings.

Kirstie Allsopp . . . As Oscar Fry once said wittily, 'Who's that ~~tubby~~ pregnant brunette drinking lager and talking to an estate agent telephonically from the best seat in the pub next to the fire?' The answer, of course, is Kirstie Allposh, beloved house-finder to the Middle Classes and third in line to the throne. It was she who found Downton Abbey for The Earl of Grantham, Brideshead for the Flytes and the windmill for Caractacus Potts in *Chitty Chitty Bang Bang* (but without the live/work planning permission he needed, which led to a rather nasty legal wrangle with the council, described in *Chitty Chitty Bang Bang II* (out of print)).

Kilts . . . It is easy to spot a Middle Class Englishman at a Scottish wedding, he will be the one wearing the Kilt. That is not to say that the Scots don't wear them themselves, they do, far too often, but an Englishman with a Scottish grandmother really has the passion for it. There is a lot of speculation regarding what should be worn under the Kilt. Traditionalists and those who consider themselves well endowed wear nothing at all, others will more modestly sport a small pair of Scottish pants known as a 'jock strap'. I play it safe and wear a whole pair of jeans under mine.

Knocking Through . . . One of the most important things you can do to say you're Middle Class is to Knock Through. The problem many Middlings are now encountering is that the house they have just bought has already *been* Knocked Through. On the surface this may appear to be good news, but actually it's very disappointing and it is hard to resist the urge to Knock Through just a little bit more. At this stage the house falls down and it is time to ring Kevin McLoud.

Kipling . . . Despite lying to get his short-sighted son a commission in the Irish Guards in World War I, where he was fatally injured within days, Kipling is something of a patron saint to children. With his wonderfully sweet Cherry Bakewells, the yielding yet crunchy Country Slices and his enduring classic the Bramley Apple Pie, his name will always be synonymous with English cakework.

Kath Cidston . . . The nemesis of superdrearoes Farrow & Ball. As soon as they coat a wall or piece of furniture with Dead Grey, along comes Kath Cidston, the Fairy Godmother of fun, who waves her wand and a shower of baby blue and pink blossoms descend on the cushions and cups which brightens the whole place up again. The dreary-drudges respond with a flurry of floor tiles in Old Bacon, and she broadsides with a tablecloth of gay cowboys. And on and on it goes . . .

Kumon . . . This is a very expensive form of extracurricular maths torture designed to make children who already don't care for maths absolutely loathe it. Tiger parents under the guise of trying to help their cub's progress through the school ranks, enrol them in Kumon classes, which means they have to spend hours every day, even on their birthday, doing sums instead of playing with ~~matches~~ computer games like normal children.

Kindling . . . When authors get fed up of trying to sign copies of their latest masterpiece on a Kindle they hurl them to the ground, where they shatter into literally quite a few shards, and those shards are called 'Kindling' (this is balls and the eBook market is important to us, Kindles and other e-readers are actually very marvellous). Kindling is really the damp and bendy grandfather of paraffin firelighters. In Middling households, where Kindling is preferred, it is a treasured commodity and is often looked after better than the family dog or rabbit. During recessions we have been known to give bags of nearly dry Kindling as Christmas presents with ~~much success~~ quite disappointing results, come to think of it.

King James Bible . . . The original Firestone and Brim version of the Bible, translated by ~~King James~~ . . . ~~God~~ . . . ~~Jesus~~ . . . some scholars and printed in the tiniest ever font (not as in font you get baptised in, typeface). It is the opposite of the guitar-strumming happy-clappy Bible and is the version particularly favoured by those Middlings who don't go to church and who can't read it anyway on account of the tiny font.

Kedgeree . . . A fishy old colonial classic that hungry Middlings have been devouring ever since the Raj and the East India Company went out of business. Serve it in a pith helmet and eat on the verandah, while reclining on a tiger-skin rug shot by Great Uncle Bulgaria. Kedgeree is one of the few all-rounder Middling dishes, that is to say, it can be served at all three conventional meals of the day, bruncheon, luncheon and ~~supcheon~~ supper.

Knitting Clubs (Stitch and Bitch) . . . Part of the thrill of being Middle Class is to be able to do the old-fashioned things your grandparents did but in a modern, vaguely ironic way. Hence the resurgence of knitting. It's not enough to do it at home on your own, in front of Channel 4 Racing; to appreciate the irony properly you need to make it a group activity. Another popular female hobby is ~~gossiping~~ bitching, and what better way to while away an evening with your chums than in combining the two — stitching and bitching. The combination is almost as clever as slippers and socks — slippersocks! The only problem is, that rather like with book clubs, the hosting can all get a bit competitive . . .

Kelims . . . These are ethnic fabric coverings, not to be confused with plain old rugs, and are very popular amongst Middlings. We use them to cover our floors, coffee tables, chairs, slippers, pencil cases and poofs, not as in gays, but in the modern sense of the word, a cushiony foot thing.

Kitchen Suppers . . . The new name for Middle Class dinner parties and particularly apt now that we have knocked down all the dining-room walls and it is impossible to eat in a downstairs room that doesn't have a kitchen in it somewhere. Don't take a Middling at their word when they say, 'Oh, do come over for a Kitchen Supper, in the kitchen, terribly informal of course, don't bother washing or changing or anything . . .' If you do as they say, you will get awfully grubby fingermarks on their best damask napkins and not be invited back.

L is for the Last Night of the Proms...

LAST NIGHT OF the PROMS

It's the last night of the Proms

They say that every year

Labrador . . . The winner of the 'Best in Middle Class' category at every year's Crufts and now the world's first canine 'brand'. First came the Labradoodle, a hybrid between a Labrador and ~~an absent-minded drawing~~ a Poodle, and soon other spin-offs will be spun out all over the Poshwolds. Next spring will see the arrival of the Labrananny and the Labrahoover (which can clear a table with one sweep of its tail), and the following year the eagerly anticipated Labradoor which will revolutionise the way we come in and out of rooms.

Lent . . . Lent sounds very like Lindt, which is confusing as the only thing Middlings are *not* allowed to think about at Lent is *Lindt*, which the Bible clearly bans us from having anything to do with for forty days and forty nights. Very few of us have any idea why, but we follow the rules religiously and then, come Eatser (*sick*) Day, we gorge ourselves silly on it — but obviously, only if it is shaped like an egg . . . or a bunny.

Lurchers . . . In the old days, when people's eyes often pointed in different directions, gypsies used to give Lurchers away in pubs. Now you can only buy them at great expense from women called Horatia who will have to come and inspect your home, your second home, your French farmhouse *and* your Teepee before she lets you have one of her precious ~~killers~~ puppies. Once you have your Lurcher you must then buy up all the farms surrounding your properties to make sure your expensive psychopath isn't shot by angry farmers within the first week.

Latin . . . It is well known to anyone who has ~~been forced at cane point~~ taken the time to master the mother of all European languages, that a working knowledge of Latin is all we need to get by in most foreign situations, particularly any that may occur in Puglia.

Land Rovers . . . Around the age of thirty-five (which is also the top speed), Middle Class men start breeding and the lure of the Vintage Land Rover really takes hold. Only other Middling men of the same age understand why.

Linen . . . Without Linen, suits, shorts, shirts and underthings it would be quite impossible for Middling men of a certain age to ever go abroad, to cricket matches, outdoor operas, picnics, barbeques or venture outside in the summer at all.

Linen   Linout

Logs . . . Ever since Mrs Thatcher did for our ~~milk~~ coal industry, Middlings have had to burn Logs. Which is fine, but where do all the children suddenly disappear to when your chimney needs sweeping? The other problem is where to put the Logs now the Log Shed has been converted into a Scandinavian-style garden office. Luckily, quick-thinking Middlings have rebranded the Log as a wall decoration. Up and down the land we are ripping out the bookshelves and replacing them with lovely big floor to ceiling stacks of Logs. This look is such a hit it is catching on even in houses without a fireplace.

Le Creuset . . . The answer to the age-old question that has troubled Middlings in the 3-for-1 doughnut queue outside Greggs the Bakers for generations – 'Why aren't French women fat?' – can be found in the Le Creuset cupboard. Operating a kitchen filled with incredibly heavy, weapon-grade cast-iron casseroles, griddle pans, spatulas, cafetières, whisks and potato peelers keeps one as trim and toned as an athlete. If Edif Piath hadn't been a regular user of Le Creuset she would never have been known as the 'Little Sparrow' but the rather less romantic-sounding 'Chubby Capon'.

Lumpfish roe . . . 'There are lots of good reasons for going to parties, but lumpfish roe isn't one of them,' *Oscar Fry*. However, we have discovered that the reason why Middlings have a mania for sprinkling Lumpfish Roe on everything from omelettes to Eton mess is in the hope of actually eating the lumpfish to extinction. Thanks to underwater nature documentaries we have seen how goppingly ugly they are and the last thing we want is for Passionfruit and Victorinox to get frightened to death by one when snorkelling off the coast of Norway during their gap year.

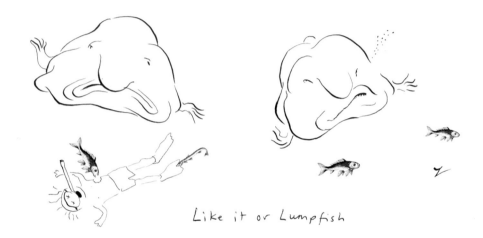

Like it or Lumpfish

Loo . . . Middlings see the walls of the Loo as somewhere we can show off without appearing boastful. For even though it could be construed as conceited to have framed our 'Italic Writing, Under 12s, South of England' third-place certificate, the context of the Loo, where we've hung it, is an indication to those who are quick to judge that at heart we are modest and quite able to cock a wry snook at our own startling achievements. The Loo is also very convenient for catching up on a bit of reading. We managed to finish *War and Peace* in one sitting (a visit to the doctor did follow). The best book for the Loo is of course ~~*Schott's Miscellany*~~ *The Middle Class ABC*, which ~~irritatingly~~ intentionally is not *quite* small enough to fit round the bend, should its relentless mix of ~~witty gags and hilarious cartoonery~~ awful puns and artless doodles leave you flushing with rage.

Libraries . . . Often confused with a loo, as they have almost as many books, but generally more places to fall asleep as they are usually ~~quiet quite~~ quite quiet and it can be all too easy to nod off till closing time (or is that the pub?). Anyway, some people called the Government have decided that if you haven't paid attention and learned enough at school, you shouldn't be encouraged to sit around all day reading books so are busy closing them down.

Light . . . Just like moths, Middlings are drawn to the Light, and Light can be found in some surprising and easy-to-book (cheap) destinations. So if friends are rude enough to question your new-found love of Bolton, Neath or Grimsby, just start murmuring, 'Oh, but the Light . . . the Light over that post-Victorian industrial landscape it is *utterly* sublime.' The only problem is that you may find the Boutique Travel Lodge fully booked next time you plan a minibreak.

Larders . . . Experiments in jam cooking, chutney boiling, ketchup mashing and sloe ginning take up most of the space in Middling Larders. What's left is given over to tins of beans bought in 'charming little old-fashioned groceries in Puglia', cassoulet from Gascony and some bratwurst Grandpa brought back from the war in 1945. Only a visit from the Food Standards Agency or a nuclear holocaust will clear them out.

M is for Maldon Salt...

Midwinter in Middletown

Manners . . . No one would deny that Middlings are 'to the manners born' or that 'mannerth maketh Middle Clath man and woman'. The problem is other people. It's no good going out there armed with good intentions; this will only land you in trouble, and possibly hospital . . .

Marmalade Making . . . Traditionally, there are two types of Middle Class Marmalade. Ma-malade, which is really easy to make and only needs Seville oranges, sugar, a pan, a saucer in the freezer and a few old jam jars; and Pa-malade, which is a different kettle of fish. For Pa-malade you will need: Seville oranges, eight pans, sugar, triple-strength pectin, a thermometer, setting points, a boiler suit, goggles, wellingtons and Heston Bloomingtall on standby.

Marks & Spencer . . . A beloved Middle Class institution without which we wouldn't have any undies or ovaries (that doesn't sound right). Anyway, the drawing below shows just how important a good slogan is to a burgeoning business . . .

Mozart . . . Provider of lovely symphonies, sonatas, movie soundtracks, advertising jingles and, more nutritiously, marzipan balls, Mozart has been top of the pops with Middlings since records began. Recently, however, his sales have slipped due to Mozartitis, an allergy that affects young Middlings, brought on by having 'Eine Kleine Nachtmusik' blasted at them in the womb morning, noon and nacht. The afflicted can be spotted rushing from weddings, funerals, films and adverts with their fingers in their ears.

Marinating . . . It took a couple of generations of Middlings Marinating themselves in Badedas for the penny to drop that this might work on food as well. It is now an unspoken rule that almost every piece of meat we cook should be Marinated and a properly spoken rule if it is to be barbequed. If you don't have the time to leave your meat languishing in a tub of red wine and wild garlic for a few hours, then at least rub it vigorously with paprika before spanking with rosemary and putting to the heat.

Marquees . . . However long you spend deciding whether to go for 'The Blenheim', 'The Balmoral' or the ironic '49, The Laurels', just like the turkey at Christmas, a Marquee will either be too big or too small. Neither is good. If it is too big it will appear as if nobody likes you, and if it is too small everyone will think you were too mean to pay for a bigger one. If you are having a party which involves French Middlings, we'd suggest not using one at all, as it will only lead to serious social-climbing frustration if you mention there is a *Marquee* in the garden and they find out it is just a big white tent.

Meadows . . . According to historical records such as the Doomsday Book and the *Radio Times*, it used to take ten men to mow a Meadow (they were clearly doing something wrong). Now, thanks to all those marvellous gardening programmes and helpful articles in the Sunday supplements, Meadows are fashionable again, albeit in a far more streamlined 21st century way. To make one, just go on holiday to Puglia for a couple of weeks and when you come back, instead of mowing the whole lawn just cut a path through the middle and *hay pesto* (which is also a by-product), instant Meadow!

Memorial Services . . . Much more fun than funerals and terrific places to catch up with your chums without the expensive presents and B&B bother of a wedding. Best of all, there's no chance you'll be asked to another smaller, more low-key one a few years later 'because things didn't really work out'.

Microplane Graters . . . Originally invented to shred small planes, someone, probably Nutella Lawson, realised that their super-sliciness could also be effective on hard cheese and lemons. As you would expect from something sharp enough to reduce aeronautical-grade titanium to tinsel, it can, and often does, make mincemeat out of fingers.

Midges . . . It is dreadful luck for Scotland, with all its Bens, Butts and Beauty that each year in the twenty minutes it has for summer — when the driving drizzle stops, the sleet vaporises and the clouds rise above knee level — out pop the Midges to turn it back into hell on earth. Since before Bonnie Prince Charlie drove over the Toll Bridge to Skye, holidaying Middlings have been waging an unwinnable war on them and always embrace the latest advances in anti-midge technology.

Man Hugs . . . Modern Middling men are not content with shaking hands with our friends; it feels stiff, formal and a bit old-fashioned. We like to show our affection with a more passionate meeting of chests. There is, however, a fine line between man-to-man hugging and being gay, and those chaps who don't want to be considered gay make this clear by beating down on their fellow huggers' backs with their hands and playing them like a drum which, if you're being hugged by a proper homophobe, can hurt a bit.

Milk . . . In the old days, when we wouldn't dream of ringing each other after 8 pm, the only worry we had about Milk was whether or not the tits would have got at it first and drunk all the cream. These days, thanks to all the unwanted pregnancies and the availability of cheap DNA tests for suspicious husbands, milkmen have been banned, and because of allergies, Milk now comes from Soyas, Wheatgerms, Goats and Hemps. Of course, no self-respecting tit would want to steal *that*, even if it was left on a doorstep without a lid and a cherry floating on top. This has made life very uncomfortable for the few dairy cows there are left.

Music Lessons . . . Just before Marzipan and Ampersand have mastered hand-eye co-ordination is the time to enrol them in Music Lessons. Very few Middlings have any natural aptitude for playing music, but like eating vegetables, we know it is good for us. The most popular instrument of ~~torture~~ music is still the piano, not on account of it being any easier to learn but because a badly played piano will sound much better than a violin or trumpet, for which a soundproofed practice room is not a luxury but an essential.

Moth Hysteria . . . A tragic side effect of the Middle Class mania for owning cashmere. Having mortgaged our mortgage for a down payment on a sock, snood or fingerless glove, we find ourselves engaged in an impossible battle with an almost invisible enemy. Our first line of defence is spraying the entire house and garden with mothballs. When that doesn't work, we fell a cedar forest and plank it into shelving and cupboards. But when those *damned* little holes *still* appear in our favourite balaclava, we buy a chest freezer and move into it wearing every piece of cashmere we own. Luckily, the psychiatric ward in the local hospital is completely clothes-moth free.

Museums . . . Once, for Poppadom and Buttermilk, a trip to the Museum involved nothing more stirring than a trudge around dusty rooms filled with maps and Magna Cartas, often without even the lure of a shrunken head on a stick to liven things up. Now, thanks to The Café Society, which has taken over all the Museums, those boring old exhibits have been banished to the basement and the uncluttered space turned into lovely cafés offering 'Digestible History' such as Mary Queen of Scotch Eggs, Blackberry and Apple Cromwell, and our favourite, Hadrian's Waffle.

My . . . The ultimate accolade a Middling can bestow upon a tradesman is to claim him as our own and call him 'mine' . . .

Map-Reading Arguments . . . The invention of the Cat Sat on the Mat Nav hasn't come soon enough to save the many thousands of Middle Class marriages lost to Map-reading Arguments. No one quite knows why it causes such disproportionately ferocious and bitter disagreements, but it does. The situation is not helped by the fact that men are incapable of asking strangers for directions, and women always think that the map itself is actually wrong.

Meditation . . . Meditation is quite Middle Class. Now there's something (not) to think about . . .

 **is for the Naughty Step...**

The Naughty Step

The Very Naughty Step

Norfolk . . . Noel Cowardy-Custard once jokingly said that Norfolk was very flat, and ever since then, whenever anyone mentions Norfolk, the first person to wittily riposte 'very flat Norfolk' gets a ~~punch~~ . . . ~~prize~~ . . . turkey. This happens far less frequently nowadays, because Norfolk and its famous ~~marshes~~ mountains have been discovered by all the Middlings who can't fit in to Cornwall during the summer. It's such a refreshing change too, to be huddling behind our surfboards escaping the winds that lash in from the Urals instead of from the monsoons that lumber in so predictably from the Atlantic.

Nannies . . . After hiring a cleaner to keep your house in order, next on the list is a Nanny to do the same for your children. If you are lucky enough to find a good one, hire her on the spot, even if you don't have any children. This should free you up to get on with really important Middle Class things like starting a charity to help children whose parents are hardly ever at home and are brought up by people they aren't related to and don't know very well, which is a dreadful problem nowadays, apparently.

Nigella . . . Nutella Lawson is the siren who first lured Middle Class men into the kitchen. Without her we would never have considered cooking in our underwear, pouting at the fridge, shimmying past the island or sitting swinging our legs on the tumble dryer while dribbling chocolate down our chins in the middle of the night.

Wake up! You're panting ...and dribbling

Names . . . 'A name is for life, not just for christenings' *Oscar Fry*. Wise words from the man who wrote *The Importance of Being Lady Windolene's Fanbelt*. When Ptolemy and Ptarmigan the ptwins, who have been the talk of family parties because their Names are 'such fun and so original', go to school and realise they have got major competition in that department from the likes of Verdana, Euphorbia, Squirrel, Peritonitis, Cornucopia and Ettall, they are left with no alternative but to change their names by Deed Poll to Jane and John.

National Anthem . . . This is the Queen's favourite song and she never gets bored of hearing it. It is a bit strange, though, that however many times she has heard it she still hasn't learned the words and never joins in. (A bit like the England football team, now we come to think of it . . .)

Nelson . . . It is entirely factual, true and borne out by facts that if you are Middle Class and want your son to have a career as a hero you must call him Nelson. If you don't believe us, two words: Admiral Nelson and Nelson Mandela. It's a shame that they never met, because as well as having the same name they both endured so much hardship. Admiral Nelson lost most of his eyes, arms and legs and Nelson Mandela had to meet the Spice Girls.

Nettle Soup . . . If your Middle Class credentials are ever questioned, a hearty panful of Nettle Soup soon silences any doubters. The making of it ticks so many Middling boxes: it is weeding with a purpose, organic, involves foraging and has been marinated (in fox pee). However, unless you are in a very bad mood, do fight the urge to garnish with fresh nettle leaves.

Nests of Tables . . . There are few sadder sights in a Middle Class house than these unloved Nests of Tables, forced to huddle together for warmth and affection. They know they are on borrowed time and that only the keen eyes of the vintage members of the family, by whom they were given in the first place, ensures their survival and keeps them out of the charity shop or kindling box.

I am *completely* mystified as to how they got in there, Auntie. I can only think our cleaner must have gone nuts. I'll fire her on Monday

Kindling

Nests . . . If you are a Middle Class child, it is inevitable that one day when you're playing Angry Birds on your iThing, a grandparent will get the wrong end of the stick and think that you are actually interested in birds and drag you outside to look for Nests. They will tell you thrilling of stories of how as children they scampered up elm trees to remove the eggs of a Little Auk (now extinct), to take pride of place in their rare bird egg collection. It is very important that you show NO INTEREST whatsoever. Showing interest will mean that every birthday or Christmas from then on, all you will be given are bird books, bird board games, birdsong CDs, bird feeders, bird tables and really embarrassing bird T-shirts and it won't even stop when you get married: your present will be a ~~Ford Thunderbird~~ bird bath.

Name Tapes . . . Because teaching girls to sew is ~~sexy~~ sexist, it has been banned in schools so now no one knows how to do it. Usually this doesn't matter, but on 31st August every year all the chickens come home to roost in one basket when Name Tape season starts. Peppermint and Mortadella, with their fifteen hundred items of uniform between them including fencing hats, lax pants, bee-keeping culottes and three grades of plimsoll (indoor, outdoor and stiletto) must both arrive at St Yoghurts with Name Tapes attached by HAND SEWING only.

← bee keeping culottes

Napkin Rings . . . In the very old days, when the world was still flat and men wore skirts, all the best and cleverest people in the kingdom got together and held a council to decide what would be the most ~~mind numbingly boring~~ edifying present to give Middle Class children for their christenings. William the Conqueror suggested a coal scuttle and Boudicca a toast rack, but it was King Cnut who swept the floor with his suggestion, a Napkin Ring. To this day, godparents who give engraved silver Napkin Rings as christening presents are referred to affectionately as ~~Cnuts~~ thoughtful.

Nappies . . . Like pasta, Nappies used to be made by hand and were often covered with an unappetising-looking sauce. Thank goodness for progress. Now, no sooner has Topiary bobbed to the surface of the birthing pool than she is measured up for her first set of organic, biodegradable, double-gusseted, squeeze-dry, lemon-scented, bottom-moisturising, wipe-clean, temperature-controlled, super-comfi, dri-fit, portable baby biodigesters. (Sadly this level of development hasn't been matched by the pasta industry, which since the ground-breaking invention of ravioli has rather taken its fettucini off the pedal.)

Baby circa 1960

present day

Nostalgia . . . As J. R. Hartley pointed out in the first sentence of his masterpiece *Fly Fishing*, 'The past is another country, but EasyJet doesn't fly there.' This is bad news for Middlings. Apart from Puglia, Nostalgiashire is the place they'd most like to go to. It's a lovely sunny upland filled with people in pubs drinking the Dunkirk Spirit out of Toby Jugs, helping Dame Vera Lynn roll out the barrels over the White Cliffs of Dover and doing the Hokey Cokey in and out of each other's houses while the Kray Twins drive around in Inspector Morse's Jaguar making sure no one is scrumping apples in Ma Larkin's orchard, where Bonnie Prince Charlie is hiding up a tree singing 'Greensleeves'. Perfick.

Rosé tinted glasses

 is for Owls...

Barn Owl

Barn Conversion Owl

Olive Oil . . . Were you to have been cryogenically frozen in the 1970s, then defrosted in the present day (unlikely, we grant you), the most striking thing to strike you, other than the lack of flying cars, would be the availability of Olive Oil. Back then it was a merchandising spin-off from *The Popeye Show* and only available in chemists as an ear medicine. Today it is even more popular than lard! There is almost nothing Middlings don't do with it, from massage to sausage, from salad lubricant to dinner-party present. It is what keeps our hearts beating healthily and our wheels turning smoothly. It would not be going too far to say that our culture is completely ~~saturated~~ unsaturated with it.

Oatcakes . . . When Middlings say, in that rather patronising way we do, that apart from their delicious deep-fried Mars bars and sausage-coated eggs, the Scots haven't got a clue about healthy eating, we say one word, ~~McDonalds~~ Oatcakes! They are the perfect diet food. We burn up a million calories chewing them and then another million as we fiddle about with our tongues trying to dislodge all the bits and pieces that have got stuck in our teeth.

Otters . . . It is a cause of great delight to Middlings that the Otter is once again frolicking about in the nation's rivers. Problems lie ahead, however, because as *their* numbers rise, trout numbers move in the opposite direction. It is only a matter of time before troutraged fishermen start shaking their fists and calling them *rotters*, get them re-re-classified as pests and start ~~hunting them again~~ managing the population.

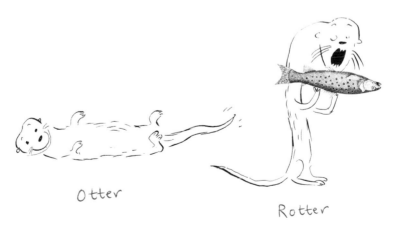

Otter

Rotter

Obituaries . . . There is nothing a Vintage Middling likes better than opening the paper, reading the Obituaries and discovering their favourite brother, sister, ex-husband or wife has died. Shortly after the glow of realising they have outlived their nearest and dearest wears off, Obit Envy sets in and they spend the rest of the day worrying that theirs won't be as prominent – or as praiseworthy.

Orchards . . . Were it not for Orchards, Sir Isaac Walton would never have discovered ~~grave robbing~~ gravity and we would still be floating about like spacemen. Compared to his eventful picnic, nothing much has happened in an Orchard since then. However, they do have a strong appeal to Middlings. We need only bury a couple of apple cores in the garden to feel justified in referring to it from then on as 'The Orchard'. The last thing a Middling wants is a *real* Orchard; the blossom stage is fun but annoyingly the trees go on to produce hundreds and thousands of apples, which we have absolutely no idea what to do with. We can't bear to leave them rotting on the ground, but there's only so much apple crumble a family can eat or cider it can drink.

Overdrafts . . . A bit like herpes, once you've got one they are awfully hard to get rid of; but unlike herpes, it is fine to talk about them at dinner parties. It's what sets us apart from Americans (as well as bone size) who love to talk about how much money they have. We Middlings like to talk about how much money we haven't. Of course in these times of financial awkwardness it is of great comfort to us to know that the people with the biggest Overdrafts of all are not the Properly Posh but the banks themselves, so reassuring.

Offal . . . However often Hugh ~~Furry Wholesale~~ . . . ~~Furtively Witty~~ . . .Heston tries to get us excited about eating Offal, Middlings find it offally hard to swallow. It is, however, very useful for getting rid of our unwanted weekend guests or relations. Just the mention of salmon gizzard pie, artichoke and tripe dip or calves liver ice cream for lunch will have them ~~retching~~ reaching for their car keys and rushing back to London early 'to beat the traffic'.

Obelisks . . . Almost all Middlings develop green fingers at around the age of forty. However many doctors we see, and however hard we wash them, there is nothing we can do about this, it is just another glorious fact of Middle Class life. The few who miss out on this ~~affliction~~ gift but still want to participate in life outdoors plant Obelisks, which earn you a lot of appreciation yet don't require any of the green-fingered hocus-pokery needed to tell apart the weed from the very much non-weed.

Outside . . . Italy has its gorgeous rolling Outside (*al fresco*, we like to call it) where long Proseccoey lunches are punctuated by the sound of Poppin and Jodhpur joyfully playing hide and seek in the cypresses, safe from paedophiles, who simply don't happen there. France has the almost as nice *en plein air* where baguettey picnics on Kith Cadston rugs, and if you're lucky, a bit of hanky panky happen. Back home in Blighty, our Outside is usually drizzly, there are paedophiles with binoculars in every bush and Poppin and Jodhpur won't get out of the car (unless they are bribed with a banker sized bonus) to go for a walk.

Orthodontists . . . These are a bit like regular dontists but more Middle Class and more expensive (it *is* possible). Strangely, it's not like pulling teeth getting Pugin and Cuckoo to go to one; they aren't in the least bit frightened of them. It is the parents who get sweaty palms and shallow of breath as they walk through the pearly white marble foyer, thinking about having to sell the barn conversion in the Poshwolds to pay for Cuckoo's underground railway tracks and Pugin's invisible titanium head brace.

Ottomans . . . Every year the Ottoman carries off the prestigious *World of House Magazine* prize for 'The Most ~~Irritating~~ Versatile Piece of Furniture Ever Invented'. Neither a seat nor a cupboard, it is sort of both while being neither. It is best plonked in the middle of a room and filled with DVDs, games, old golf balls, jigsaws and dust. On the top, where you *could* sit, put back issues of *Country Life* from 1973, an abdication copy of *The Times* and all the books too big to fit in the bookcase. If you ever doubt your Middle Classness, go and stand before it; *so* empiring.

Organic . . . For centuries cannibals have been sitting down to their dinner secure in the knowledge that what they were eating was free of pesticides, poisons, fertilizers and hormones. Irritatingly for them this is no longer the case. From our nylon tracksuits and fizzy pop to our factor 50 suncream, we have marinated ourselves in weird chemicals. Thank goodness for the Organic movement. Its philosophy chimes completely with the Middle Class sense of fair play *and* ecomentalism. There is now nothing more healthy for a cannibal chief to eat than a young British Middling. What's more they don't even have to peel them; even their pants are Organic. For we non-cannibals, our favourite thing about organic is still that when all the fennels or aubergines or pak chois are sold out in the fruit and veg section of the supermarket, we know that we will always be able to find them on the organic shelf (and by then we will be so relieved to have our crucial ingredient that we won't mind paying ~~the little bit~~ quite a lot more for it).

Oysters . . . Middlings ~~love~~ . . . ~~hate~~ . . . have a love–hate relationship with Oysters. We love their aphrodisiacal powers and reminiscing about the old days when they were bought for tuppence ha'penny a barrel and were the food of the poor. We hate the fact that there is a tiny chance we will eat a bad one that will leave us writhing in agony for days with an acute case of runny tummy. It's like Russian roulette for the Middle Classes, but with much better odds . . . and erotic side effects.

P is for Pronunciation...

Placement (Pronounced Frenchily) . . . At Middling dinner parties there will always be one couple who aren't talking to each other, another couple who aren't talking to anyone apart from each other, another who can't talk to anyone because they have drunk too much by the time they sit down, another who are too scared to talk to anyone at all and finally a couple who simply won't shut up. If you happen to have a black belt in seating planning then none of this should be a problem. It's also worth remembering that if you go to the trouble of writing your guests' names down on little pieces of card and plonking the cards about the table, then, technically, you have moved up from a dinner party to a banquet and Toad-in-the-Hole for the main course will no longer cut the mustard.

Ping Pong . . . Popular amongst agoraphobic Middlings who like sport but can't be doing with all that running about outside nonsense, which most sport involves. Originally it was called *Ping Ping*. The name only changed in 1847 after Queen Victoria insisted on a vigorous bout of it following a state banquet for the Windward Islands consisting mainly of sprouts, Jerusalem artichokes and flageolet beans.

Panettone . . . Brilliant last-minute Middle Class Christmas present consisting of stale Italian bread studded with currants, which you can still buy in Waitrose on Christmas Eve when all the other shelves are completely empty.

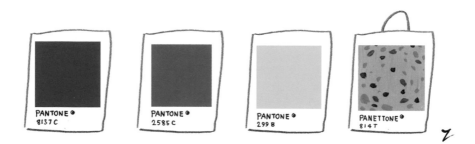

Pesto . . . Like Rome itself, Italian recipes are eternal. Pesto has been made the traditional way for centuries: young children chew basil and then spit it out into little jars. It has taken the pioneering British Middling to question the orthodoxy of only using basil. We think it's much more fun to turn *anything* flimsy and green into Pesto: wild garlic, nettles, chervil, grass clippings . . .

People Carriers . . . People Carriers are very popular with the Middle Classes. We can fit either lots of children and some of their clobber into one, or, alternatively, one child and *all* its clobber. You can easily spot them in the summer holidays causing traffic jams on the M5 on the way to Cornwall or M6 heading to Scotland. To make sure Agapanthus, d'Artagnan, Banjo and Villareal don't bother us with silly questions like, 'Are we nearly there yet?' or, 'Can we stop for a wee?', they come fitted with satellite dishes to stream live *X-Factor* updates and allow them to communicate with each other on the back seat via Twitter and Facebook, which is so much more efficient than talking.

Pony Club . . . Unlike some clubs, which apparently can be quite hard to join, it's really rather easy for Ravioli and Custard to join Pony Club. All they need is a pony, a field, a horse-box, saddles, stirrups, stables, bits, bobs, bridles, grooms, a blacksmith, dubbin, dobbin, jodhpurs, Spurs, Arsenals, whips, Range Rover/ Land Rover, haynets, hairnets (easily confused), antihisthamine pills, lunging reins, anti-lunging reins, lassoes and a good seat.

Period Dramas . . . In the old days, when the common cold could kill, we would all sink into depression on a Sunday night because looming over us was the thought that the following morning we would have to get up early and go and work down a mine. Thankfully, we now live in the modern age, those beastly mines have closed down and we're all Middle Class. Now we cheerfully spend Sunday evenings surrounded by fun cushions on our comfy sofas, watching the old days brought safely back to life on the television.

Prosecco . . . A bit like Sir Walter Raleigh's fruitful trips to America, which resulted in Elizabethan Middlings discovering the delights of ~~bicycles~~ tobacco and potatoes, more recent Middling forays to Italy have opened our mouths to Prosecco. 'I think I prefer it to Champagne, to be honest.' 'Much easier to drink on a hot afternoon.' 'I swear you can taste Tuscany in each bubble!' Of course, our new-found love for it has absolutely nothing at all to do with the fact that it is half the price of champagne – absolutely nothing at all.

Pussy willow . . .

Used to grow outside on willow trees from mid April, but now only found on Middle Class windowsills, which is much better.

Pussy Willow

Wussy Pillow

Pillow fight? No thanks

Parmesan . . .

For years Middlings assumed that Parmesan was some kind of acrid dust which came in small tubs, a flamboyant sprinkle of which over a spag-bol bestowed the finishing touch of class. Then someone actually went to Italy and discovered that it was cheese. It was instantly rebranded Parmigiano, quadrupled in price *and* we had to grate it ourselves. An interesting fact is that the hardest object in the known universe is a small lump of Parmigiano that was found last year in the door of a Middling's fridge in Lewes.

Hard cheese guys

Diamond

Belfast Sink

Pimms . . . What with globular warming, the melting of the polar bears and the blurring of the seasons, Pimms has really come into its own. Without it, Middlings would be hard-pushed to know when summer actually begins. The first sighting of a bottle on the shelves at Waitrose is the trigger to take off our corduroys and cashmere and break out the linen. The other advantage is that we no longer need to waste hours leaning over the compost bucket peeling vegetables. The average glass of Pimms served with all the trimmings contains all five of our Five-a-Day, so, 'Good health all round!'

Pudding Wine . . . A wine invented for Middle Class children. It comes in little bottles, which are easy for them to handle, and is nice and sweet to the taste. Sometimes, however, at the end of a grown-up dinner, when we have finished all our own wine, in the consequent pandemonium we do help ourselves to it. This normally leads to the Pudding Wine Game: from the first moment the words *Pudding Wine* are mentioned, time how long it is until someone says either *Botrytis* or *noble rot*; it should be no more than forty-five seconds. The next round is to ask what it means; this takes much longer than forty-five seconds.

Point-to-Points . . . What is the point of a Point-to-Point? Well, if you ever manage to weave your way through the endless rows of picnics happening in the backs of Audis, Volvos, Range and Land Rovers, you will discover that there are actually horse races taking place. And wherever there are horse races you will find gentlemen bookmakers lurking under large umbrellas, who will gladly exchange your fiver for a slip of paper which promises enormous rewards if Chocolate Eclair comes home in race number 6. We completely forget to follow the fortunes of Chocolate Eclair, however, as we become distracted by the greater struggle of trying to find the way back to our picnic and the unfinished magnum of Prosecco therein.

Poetry . . . It's one of those wonderful ~~phenomenoms~~ . . . . ~~phenomenas~~ . . . things, that Vintage Middlings may be always losing their specs or forgetting how to send a text message, but ask them to recite a poem, and lo!, out will pour poem after poem until you beg them to stop as your heart has started beating uncomfortably in iambic pentameters. Younger Middlings, schooled in a cane-free environment, can't do this, we can only navigate the first verse of the 'Owl and the Pussycat' before floundering in the shipping lanes that border the land where the Bong-Tree grows. As for *writing* Poetry, it seems somehow sadly unlikely that a modern Middling will ever write Poetry as elegant as what that which has gone before. To be a great poet requires such detachment . . .

For pity's sake Blake, lay aside the poem and fetch a pail of water

Pick Your Own . . . Picking Your Own ~~nose~~ soft fruit is the perfect Middle Class family activity. You'd also think it was win-win-win for the growers, sitting with their feet up while you do the hard work. It's not, though; if you talk to them it's whine-whine-whine. Apparently, the EU won't allow them to weigh Zulu and Cashmere before and after they've fruit-picked, and can only charge for what's in the punnet . . .damn-damn-damn!

Panamas . . . A summer treat for Middle Class heads. These were originally introduced to the UK by salmon heading home from wintering in South America. Once the Panama Canal was opened, their journey time was cut in half, leaving them much more energy to start the import—export business they had been planning for centuries: in summer they bring over Panama hats and in winter they head back dragging container loads of tweed caps.

Playdates . . . These are very important. They are the dates on which Middle Class children go to play with each other in each other's houses. Thank goodness the Americans came up with this ~~excruciating~~ elegant noun. Until the word *Playdates* was invented, no children ever did this.

Pot Pourri . . . A French-sounding substance that sets Middlings an almost impossible challenge, which is how to dust it. Controversially we're all in favour of the hoovering method, but then again we do seem to get through rather a lot of it.

Pilates . . . If yoga and zumba seem a bit too energetic, yet watching telly with a glass of rosé and a packet of ~~crisps~~ Ryvita thins is a bit too *unergetic*, then Pilates is the activity for you. It really is the best way to strengthen your ~~parquet~~ pelvic floor and kill that bit of time between morning coffee and lunch. There is another, more extreme branch of Pilates involving some equipment left over from the Crucifixion that's been welded to an executive toy. This is the version enjoyed by celebrities and is called Pontius Pilates; it's free to Middlings (or anyone, in fact) called Barabbas.

Passing Out . . . Middlings have perfected the art of Passing Out. Army ones do it at Sandhurst by marching up and down in very straight lines, sharply dressed, looking ahead and holding swords. Barmy ones do it on holiday, wobbling about with nothing on, cross-eyed, sunburned and holding on to the furniture.

Q is for Quality Time...

This is not Quality Time

This is Quality Time

Quercus Robur . . . As most of us know, this is the Latin name for the mighty oak tree. Which is very much the tree of choice for bucolic Middlings to plant on the village green when they want to commemorate one of the Queen's jubilees or victory in their fight against the council that was trying to restrict the ~~bin men~~ Refuse and Recycling Division persons to one collection a fortnight.

Quilted Jackets . . . Once upon a time it was only possible to buy Quilted Jackets in olive green or navy blue and they were for the exclusive use of farmers' wives or people called Sloane Rangers. Now that people like to stand out rather than blend in, they come in all sorts of colours, like pink. Middlings still only wear the navy and olive ones.

Quad Bikes . . . Invented by a Formula I mechanic who was bored one weekend and put a V8 engine into his ride-on-lawnmower. Today they are mostly used by teenage Middlings to ~~show off recklessly and turn their parents hair white~~ teach themselves to drive. We have heard rumours that farmers and people who actually live in the country during the week use them for work, but this is probably a charming rural myth.

Quail's Eggs . . . 'Peeling Quails' Eggs is a fiddlesome business that if at all possible you should get someone else to do.' *Oscar Fry.* The loveliest thing about a Quail's Egg is its shell, which is the first thing we remove. After that they are just small eggs. Therefore when your recipes call for Quail's Eggs, always replace with Cadbury's Mini Eggs. These are not only charmingly speckled, but you *don't* have to peel them and they are available in four lovely colours. It's quite a good thing that celery salt doesn't stick to them too well though, as the taste combination does take a bit of getting used to.

Queuing (and Tutting) . . . Middlings are really good at both. However, it is worth remembering that you *cannot* have a Queue without a Tut, but you *can* have a Tut without a Queue, though overall this is a bit of an empty experience. The most Middle Class Queue in Britain, even more than the one on the tills at John Lewis the last Saturday before Christmas, is the Queue for tickets at Wimbledon. It wins by virtue of the fact that it involves tents, bunting and the frying of venison sausages.

GAME (sausages)   **SETTEE** (inflatable)   **MATCHES** (dangerous)

Quality Street . . . Middling households which normally only ever allow 70% cocoa solid chocolate over the threshold make an exception at Christmas, when invariably someone will present them with a massive tin of Quality Street. As soon as the tin has been opened, all the purple ones and the green triangles seem to disappear, a phenomenon which has piqued the interest of Dr Dawn French.

Quinces . . . As Edward Lear knew only too well, Quinces should be eaten with a runcible spoon. Unfortunate Middlings whose profligate ancestors squandered the family silver in cockfighting pits and dotcom bubbles will tell you that runcible spoons do not exist. Those of us whose higher branches of the family tree led lives where caution prevailed know better and can sit of a late summer evening in the shade of a bong tree happily scooping away at Quinces with a monogrammed runcible and a handy chainsaw (as Quinces can be incredibly hard).

Quoits . . . In the old days before salad came in bags, when Middlings went abroad a lot so they could write letters home complaining about the terrible heat and the natives, they spent an awful lot of time on board ship. Generally, by the time they reached the Cape Verdes all the shuttlecocks, tennis balls, netballs, cricket balls, footballs, baseballs and frisbees had gone overboard. So they had to invent a game of such appalling tedium that it would ensure no one wanted to play it, and therefore no one ever lost the main tools. Quoits fitted the bill quoit well. In fact, one of the first things salvaged from *The Titanic* were twenty Quoit cases, which had never been opened.

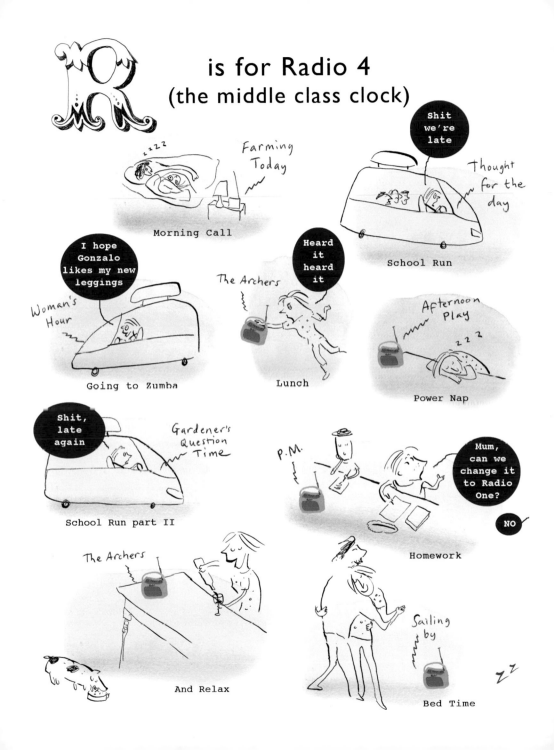

Rowing . . .

Range Cookers . . . These are all the ~~range~~ rage now in knocked-through Middle Class kitchens and essential ~~for cooking on~~ company for the American-style fridge (which can get very lonely, being so far from home on the range). They are a bit tricky to operate, however, what with the baffling amount of ovens, rotisserie attachments, in-built self-basting tandooris, wok stands, cookbook stands, wifi, deep fish fryers, shallow fish fryers, turbo waffle irons, pizza makers, soup smokers, Glühwein heaters and loads of other crêpe stuff. In fact, it is generally easier to eat out.

out of range cooker

Rocking Horses . . . Due to sensible Health & Safety requirements, these beautiful childhood toys of yesteryear can now only be used as bay window decorations. If Oak Apple *really* wants to know what it's like to ride a horse, there is probably a simulator on the Xbox station she can use in safety.

Rugby (Union) . . . A heartwarming sight on frosty Saturday mornings is the procession of Middle Class men dressed in their team colours heading out to ~~the sports fields to play~~ the gastropub to watch six nations Rugby on TV. Rugby is loved by Middle Class men throughout ~~Britain~~ England, Scotland and Ireland (in Wales it is lloved by all classes). It would be wrong of us to imply that watching it at the pub is plain lazy; it is far lazier to watch it at home. The male Middling has managed to secure Rugby-Watching the same status that Wimbledon-Watching has for women, that is to say, it exempts you from doing any housework or gardening while it is on and you can even get away with saying, *Shh!* quite loudly to anyone rude enough to talk while you're *busy* watching.

Red Kites . . . Never feed a swallow after midnight, it will turn into a Red Kite. One of the most stirring sights for Middlings hurtling up the M40 on their way to the Poshwolds are the herds of Red Kites frolicking above the carriageway. No one knows which came first – the birds or the pile-ups – but there are lots of both. Spontaneous birdwatching through a sunroof while driving at speed often ends in trouble and feeding time for the Kites. They have learned that the impact of cars colliding at velocity is enough to actually force apart the sticky lumps of travel sweets in tins, which are their favourite food.

nee naw

Rosé . . . Pink wine has been enjoyed for years by indecisive Middlings who couldn't choose between red or white so had both, mixed together, and also by very drunk Middlings at barbecues who top up their wine glasses willy-nilly from whatever bottle they could lay their hands on. We do love a compromise solution, and as compromises go, Rosé is a ~~cracker~~ winer. It would have caught on earlier had it not come from Portugal in dodgy shaped bottles. *One* of those misfortunes we could have dealt with; both, however, proved lethal to the drink's fortunes, leading to the famous refrain, 'Rosé? No way, Hosé!' These days it's rather different, as we stagger about all summer long clutching our Rosé-tinted glasses and the only dilemma for the indecisive is, 'Pink . . . or Prosecco?'

Ramekins . . . Named after Doreen, Duchess of Ramekin. Her ~~Spaceship~~ Graceship invented them to help stretch her rations to feed the seventy-three East End Evacuees who came to stay for the ~~weekend~~ war. Ever since then, ~~stingy~~ economical Middlings have used them to serve tiny portions of anything expensive to cook. It was also, of course, the invention of the Ramekin which did for the small, white British fridge. It was never going to be big enough to cope with the massive demand for space once we had tiny pots in which we could put one left-over potato or twelve left-over peas. Most Middling fridges (American style) now contain a three-figure Ramekin count of leftovers, in fascinating stages of decay, in some comfort.

Poor Celaine

Recycling . . . This time-consuming Middle Class planet-saving activity used to be known as 'putting out the rubbish'. Then it was such a simple task the cleaner was allowed to do it. Now the entire family is involved; separating the card from the cardboard, windows from envelopes, cans from can'ts, wine from bottles and the wheat from the chaffinch. Once that's all done, there's the larger items, which used to be taken to the workhouse or put on the bonfire. These we now have to drive to the ~~dump~~ Recyling Centre, where we toss all ~~last season's~~ our worn-out clothes and shoes, video cassettes and eighties pine furniture into the appropriate skips. If at this stage you fall into one yourself and land painfully on a bed of broken televisions, this is known as a 'Vicious Recycle'.

Ruins . . . There is nothing a Middling likes more than a collapsed former dwelling or derelict place of worship. It makes us feel so alive by comparison, proud of our own homes and second homes, and in the mood for a picnic.

Reels . . . These are one of the things that can happen in Scotland. The Scotch think they are reely really fun, and it is very important for the visitor to maintain this fiction. Reels are dances only the Scotch know how to do, and be warned, they like to change the rules half-way through, just when you start getting the hang of it. If you can't find a big rock with which to break both your legs before the ~~Kylie~~ Ceilidh starts, it is worth bearing in mind that a Foursome is a dance, the Gay Gordons *isn't* men only, and wearing a 'See You, Jimmy!' Tam o' Shanter is not a good idea.

Round Robins . . . Sadly the Round Robin *Erithacus rotunda* is becoming an endangered species. We, for one, will be very depressed if they disappear completely. It is entirely the fault of patronising Middlings that their numbers are in such decline, delighting as we have done in publicly ridiculing what are nothing more than generous attempts on behalf of our ~~friends and~~ acquaintances at keeping us up to date with their successes ~~and failures~~. It will be a poorer world when we can no longer laugh at Leviathan's first attempt at breaking in to the ~~neighbours' house~~ jobs market or the surprising news of a pregnancy, 'No idea how that happened!!' or Nectar's brilliant exam results, 'All A-stars! She's so clever, we often wonder if we took the right baby home from hospital!!' . . .

Rumpy Pumpy . . . This is the activity Middlings use to reproduce and occasionally throw some fun into the bargain. It is not an easy subject to penetrate, but we know it was invented in the 1960s by ~~a filthy pervert~~ a brilliant writer called D. H. Lawrence Llewellyn-Bowen. Before he came along, we reproduced ourselves with the help of someone in a missionary position (presumably a vicar) and a stork (possibly the margarine).

Roll-Top Baths . . . In the same way the Belfast Sink has triumphed over its successor, the Roll-top Bath has made such a comeback that it is now the *only* bath a modern Middling will consider. This is despite their many drawbacks: weight, price and, most importantly, lack of a ledge on which to balance your glass of Prosecco. The free-standing beauty of the Roll-top is such that we no longer feel the need to confine them to the bathroom. Boutique hotels often ~~wedge them in~~ place them tastefully in the bedroom; foodies quite often have theirs in the kitchen; ours was too heavy to make it up the stairs, so we have it in the hall.

Rare Breeds . . . There is a tipping point over which we may have tipped when the Gloucester Old Spot is found munching organic leftovers in *so* many Poshwold gardens that they can no longer be classified as a *Rare* Breed. Perhaps they, perhaps *all* 'Rare' Breeds should be renamed 'Middle Class breeds'? After all, they do tend to live charmed lives in thatched barns and organic orchards strung with bunting, and a Middling who keeps animals is always going to go for the unusual or old-fashioned variety. As ~~Jedward~~ George Orwell once wrote, 'All animals are equal, but rare breeds are more equal than others.'

Runny Tummies . . . This very unfortunate condition only affects Middlings who have ignored convention and foolishly gone to a developing (not as in photographs, that doesn't happen anywhere anymore) country, and ordered salad, watermelon or a drink with ICE IN IT! (durrr!). If you get a Runny Tummy everyone else will be very cross, especially if the time they were expecting to spend looking at ruins and views is now spent looking for loos. Follow our advice and take your own ice with you when you go on holiday, to make sure you aren't the party pooper.

Religion (C of E) . . . In the old days Middlings went to church not only at Christmas and Easter but every Sunday, because we were rather keen on God and wanted to go to heaven. These days, regular attendance at church not only guarantees you a spot in heaven but also a place for Silo and Butterdish at the attached Ofsted triple-star Primary School, which, if we're honest, is rather more important. The only other way to pack out a church these days is to host *Songs of Praise*: attending that won't get you into heaven but should get you on to BBC2, which is similar.

Re-Gifting . . . An inevitable part of modern Middle Class life due to the fact that we all have so much stuff already, yet ~~capitalism~~ convention requires us to keep on giving. Think of Re-gifting as present recycling, if the expression makes you wince. The most closely guarded place in the Middle Class home is no longer Mamma's jewellery box, it is the present drawer. It would be a catastrophe were a friend to chance upon it and find within those carefully chosen lambswool (*not* cashmere) fingerless gloves they'd given you, which you'd said had been stolen from your handbag in Florian's. We know of one packet of Bendicks Bittermints which were taken to sixty-four different Sunday lunches before actually being opened, by which time they tasted rather bitter.

Red Trousers . . . Only Mountain Rescue, Father Christmas and possibly Micky the Mouse look more ravishing in Red Trousers than the Middle Class male. The material of choice is normally corduroy, but there is a variety of reddy-pink nautical trouser which is also extremely effective. There are two reasons why a man wears Red Trousers: either to show that he has been caught for drink driving, or that he has cheated on his wife but has been forgiven and they're soldiering on for the sake of the grandchildren. If you have committed *both* faux pas, you must wear yellow trousers.

 is for Scotch Eggs...

Shooting . . . Spending Saturday morning queuing at the organic free-range butcher is a hallowed Middle Class tradition, but there is another even more time-consuming and expensive way of getting hold of organic free-range food. Shooting it. Shooting is a game for tweed-clad alpha Middlings of both the male and female varieties, which involves potting as many birds as possible. Unfortunately, though, when you collect your birds at the end of the day, they aren't in those nice polystyrene trays and covered in clingfilm but are still wearing their feathers and wings and require all sorts of work before they can be put in the oven. One way to avoid this messy job is to only shoot clay pigeons, but they really don't taste so good.

Clay Pigeon Pie

Spaniels . . . *Springers* and *Cockers* are the two sorts of Spaniels Middlings are most attracted to. Both are equally ~~annoying~~ endearing. Since the success of Dolly the Labradoodle, genetic dog combining has become very popular, but we think that however much we love Spaniels it would be a mistake to try and combine the Springer and Cocker. As much as we may cross our fingers and hope for a *Sprocker*, we could easily end up with a *Cockspring*, and nobody would want one of those.

'Sorry' . . . Even though Elton John has now been promoted to Dame, we think he may not be Middle Class at all. He seems to think that 'Sorry' is the hardest word. Honestly! All we can say is he's clearly never played doubles . . . or frisbee . . . or bumped trollies in Waitrose.

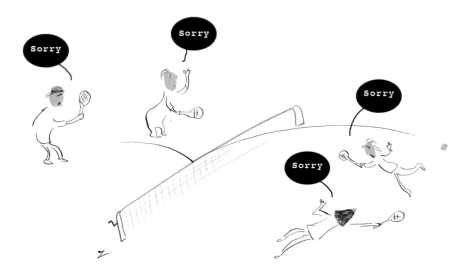

Supermarkets Abroad . . . We can't imagine life without Waitrose until, that is, we are in Puglia, Tuscany, Umbria or Gascony where we are overwhelmed by the wonderfulness of the local supermarkets, and can buy things even Waitrose doesn't sell. We load the car up with hand-sewn raviolis, cleaning products that are banned in Britain, extra-unpasteurized cheese, tins of confit and several sizes of saucisson and head home. After we have been arrested and fined by the UK Border Agency for importing dangerous foodstuffs, we swear we'll never be unfaithful again.

Shells . . . Middlings love collecting Shells, particularly from beaches which have signs saying 'leave only footprints, take only memories'. They make such wonderful bathroom mirror decorations and the ones with holes in can be strung together to form organic necklaces. If this doesn't quite satisfy your craving for danger, then head for a battlefield with a metal detector. Shells from the Somme, Austerlitz, Waterloo and Monte Cassino can easily be found, cleaned off and used as paperweights or doorstops. The excitement factor with both types resides in the question: 'Are they still live?'

Smoking . . . Now that Smoking has been banned everywhere (apart from outside pubs and office blocks, where it is mandatory), we rather miss that smoky smell, which used to permeate everyone and everything. Middlings have come up with a brilliant solution. We have knocked ~~through~~ down all our decking and gazebos and replaced them with home smokers, tandoors and outdoor pizza ovens. Once these are fully operational, everything within a radius of three miles gets a thorough kippering and all is well again with the world.

Scarves (five ages of) . . . We Middlings go into wraptures about scarves and as Oscar de la Fry once whispered (but loudly enough for everyone to hear) in a witty aside at Paris Fashion Week, 'I think of them not so much as Scarves, more as bunting for the neck.'

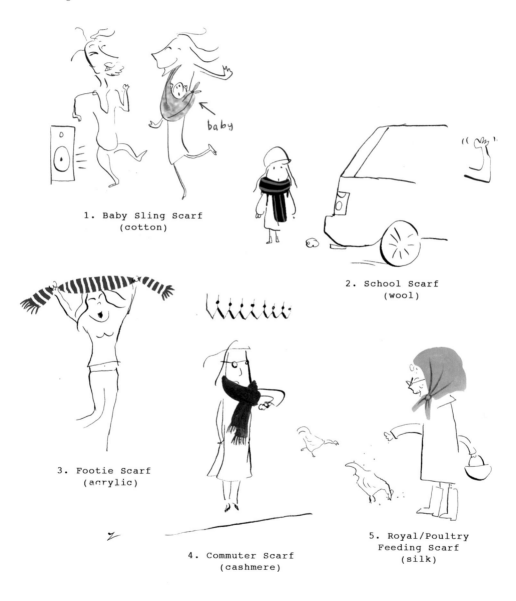

1. Baby Sling Scarf
   (cotton)

2. School Scarf
   (wool)

3. Footie Scarf
   (acrylic)

4. Commuter Scarf
   (cashmere)

5. Royal/Poultry
   Feeding Scarf
   (silk)

Sailing . . . Web-footed Middlings for whom the annual booze cruise to Calais isn't quite enough, often turn into Yotties. This is a shame, because once they have become a Yotty they simply can't have interesting conversations about the important things in life; school fees, the traffic on the M4 on Friday afternoons or whether Montenegro really is the new Puglia. Instead, all they can bang on about is the cost of moorings, the difficulty of getting in and out of the Hamble on a rip tide; that wasn't you who was stupid enough to park on the slipway, was it? And *yes*, isn't that your Audi floating past the windo . . .

Silver . . . The ultimate Middle Class crime is to ~~replace your lawn with astroturf~~ sell the family Silver. Despite possessing cupboards full of the stuff and having to clean it every Christmas morning, it is not something we ever truly own (or use). Like a large nose or bulbous eyes, 'The Silver' is something to pass on to the next generation. You will never be forgiven if you sell it; succeeding generations will not write your biography and have it privately published. For those of us desperate for cash to pay for the ~~boob job~~ school fees, the honourable thing to do is to stage a break-in. If your insurance company pays up then you can quip, 'Every cloud has a silver lining', which could earn you a reputation as a minor wit within the family and you may yet get that biography.

Scooters . . . As soon as Fresco and Jaguar are done with crawling they are ~~walking~~ scootering. This is not as alarming as it sounds, because due to childhood obesity and the support of Gillette, Scooters now come with a generous three, rather than a hopelessly old-fashioned two, ~~blades~~ wheels. The added stability this gives them is but a crumb of comfort to the anxious parents, who still encase their darlings in safety wear so cumbersome they make bomb disposal protection suits look like lycra leotards.

Scented Candles . . . Thank goodness Jo Malone Ranger rode into town and brought ~~Tonto~~ Scented Candles with her. Without them the 'signature scent' in most Middle Class homes would be the welcoming waft of chicken stock still simmering on the AGA. Be very careful buying French Scented Candles, not only do they jumble up the letters on the label, their parfumieres come up with some extraordinary flavours, vaguely familiar but not always pleasant.

I could've sworn I took the stock off the Aga yesterday

Salad . . . Before salad bags came along containing lovely Salads in a microclimate of ~~chloroform~~ chlorine, hardly anyone ever ate the stuff. It was out of the question for vegetarianists on account of all the slugs and caterpillars hiding in it and for the rest of us, those enormous floppy leaves that wrapped themselves around our chins as we struggled to fold them into our mouths were something best fed to the pet rabbit or tortoise. These days Middle Class salad bowls overflow with baby rockets, watercresses, ~~gravel~~ toasted nuts, ~~frisbees~~ frisées, edible flowers, ripped Italian peach halves and pomegranate seeds, all immaculately dressed in designer Italian silks (Balsamico and Olive Oilio). There is almost as much ~~junk~~ goodness in a Middle Class Salad as a jug of Pimms! We will look back at these days and call them Salad Days.

Schools . . . Once it was very easy to find a School for Henry and Camilla and to leave them there happily scoffing Spangles and Toffos in the tuck shop and drinking cider behind the bike shed until they were old enough to go to university. Nowadays, for Boater and Finial, what with Champions' League Tables, A-Star Academies, Paedophiles, Catchment Areas and Coursework, it's a bit more complicated. And if all that wasn't bad enough, choosing the wrong School for your children can completely ruin ~~their chances of ever getting a job~~ *your* Middle Class credentials.

Sunday Papers . . . On Sunday mornings in Middletown, just above the low hum of mowing and the clink of ice tumbling into Bloody Marys, you can hear the question, 'Anything in the papers today?' and the slightly grumpy reply, 'No, nothing; nothing at all, unless you want to see a photograph of someone's child waving at you from their tree house?' Obviously we don't actually need papers to read the news, now we have Kindle pads, cleverphones, computers and whatforth. But the gizmos are absolutely useless when it comes to drying out boots, lighting fires, cleaning windows, laying out apples, lining drawers, wrapping up broken glass, making papier-mâché masks and the many other things we like to do at the weekend — all of which a full edition of the Sunday Papers is perfect for.

Signet Rings . . . Like antelopes, Middlings find safety in numbers, so for the Middling dumped in a nudist colony as a prank on his stag night there is little that is more reassuring than the glimpse of a fellow nudist sporting a Signet Ring. If nothing else, it will be someone Middle Class to play nude tennis with until he can remember who he is, find some clothes and escape.

Cygnet Rings

Skiing . . . If the thought of hurtling down a mountain at 1,520 mph, your feet strapped to a pair of rulers, with only a ~~pint~~ half litre of Gluhwein and a bucket of melted cheese to greet you at the bottom, fills you with joy, then you must ~~need more lithium~~ be a fan of Skiing. You are not alone; there are many Middlings who can't come to terms with Christmas being over. We miss the tree, we miss the mulled wine and we totally missed the snow. Where can you find all those things in abundance *and* Toblerones galore? The mountains of Europe.

Sheepskins . . . As is well documented, in the very old days, when human beings were wild, we gave birth directly on to the backs of live sheep. Presumably as a sort of continuation of this ancient practice, modern Middlings allow newborn babies to sleep *only* on fresh cream Sheepskins.

Sherry . . . From Great Aunt Bagpuss sipping Bristol Cream in Haywards Heath to young Baskerville knocking back a chilled Fino in Soho while he waits for his tapas, Sherry is the most maligned of Middle Class tipples. In the old days, when you could put things on top of your telly, a tiny glass of warm, stale sherry was drunk by Middlings before Sunday lunch. It is a tradition that we hope doesn't return soon, as we have just taken all our dusty little goblets to Oxfam and it would be bloody typical . . .

Sloe Gin or Vodka . . . Surely one of the most popular of all autumnal Middle Class activities is picking sloes for the gin or vodka. It involves all the usual Middle Class favourites: walking, wellies, alcohol and storage jars. Unfortunately, once made it becomes the devil of a test of patience. The self-disciplined are able to hold off for the full term (9–10 months) as the flavour and colour deepen, most people get stuck in by Christmas and alcoholics by Sunday night. It is fine to receive Sloe Gin as a present, but to buy a ready-made version is *not* a good idea.

You're supposed to leave it for longer than an hour!

Slow gin

Fast gin

Swimming Pools . . . There are two types of Middling: those who have Swimming Pools, and those who know someone reasonably close by who does. It is far preferable to be the latter. It does seem bonkers to have a Swimming Pool in our climate, as it is rarely warm enough to lie around next to it, which is the chief pleasure they afford. It is rather like having an enormous invalid in the garden. They require constant monitoring, daily medicines, hoovering, heating, tucking up for the night and children aren't allowed around them unsupervised.

Swallows . . . What with their penchant for winter sun and love of travel, Swallows are clearly very Middle Class indeed. In our general state of impatience, few Middlings have bothered listening to the end of Oscar Fry's famous expression, 'One swallow doesn't make a summer'. The full version goes: 'One swallow doesn't make a summer but it does if it's *Pimms* you're swallowing.' (Pimms should be paying us for this, they aren't, but they should be). It was of course a Swallow who pecked all the jewels out of the statue of the Happy Prince and gave them to the poor. It is for this very reason that you will never see our own happy Prince of Charles wearing any prominent jewellery outdoors during Swallow season.

Sports Day . . . As we all know, Sports Day, under the cover of being an opportunity for Galantine and Pipistrel to show off their hand-eye-foot co-ordination while jumping along in a sack balancing a hard-boiled egg on a spoon, is actually only about the Mothers' Race. It is finally an opportunity to put all the yoga, zumba, Pilates and anabolic steroids to the test.

School run . . . Apart from their dress size, how much their house is worth and how much their husbands earn, the thing Middle Class Mummies lie about most is how much they dislike doing the School Run. In fact, apart from ~~lusting after~~ dancing along with Gonzalo the zumba instructor, the School Run is the absolute high point of their day. It is amazing what secrets an eight-year-old will blab about their mummy and daddy's drinking, fighting, finances, marriage, jobs and affair with the au pair, in the right environment.

Smoothies . . . Apart from Champagne and Diesel, these are the most expensive liquids on the planet. Despite attempts by Middle Class Mummies to convince Quartet and Shelduck that they are allergic to Smoothies, someone will inevitably give them one and from that first sip they'll be hooked. From then on they will lead you straight to the Smoothie aisle in Waitrose and refuse to budge until you have filled up your ~~credit card~~ trolley with bottles of the stuff. Your only chance of avoiding bankruptcy is to show them a photograph of Roger Moore – Mr Smoothie himself – in the hope that the prospect of turning out like him frightens them enough to stop.

Strawberry Pots . . . These are like regular Middle Class terracotta pots but with holes in, the intention being that infant strawberry plants are inserted into the openings. You will do this sooner than you think as when left empty they have a morose, accusing look that can be quite disconcerting.

A high count of terracotta pots, of the strawberry variety and otherwise, in a garden (or outside room) is a good indication of solid Middle Class inhabitants within. Contrarily, so is a terrace completely devoid of pots; these days the decent frost-proof, handmade ones cost even more than a Fairtrade Mexican hammock or a sustainable teak swing-ball set and, as a result, a lot get pinched by ~~green-fingered~~ light-fingered intruders.

Storage Space . . . Calamitously, it turns out that there *is* actually a drawback to our craze for knocking through (other than the house falling down) and that is the loss of Storage Space. Once every attic, cellar, larder and fuse-box cupboard have been turned into airy modern living space, there is nowhere left to actually put anything. Luckily (but only sort of) Ikea and Tina Turner sell large stackable plastic boxes or, if we're feeling nostalgic, we can buy distressed 'antique' trunks in which to store our tapestry unicorn cushions until they come back into fashion again. This won't happen, but at least a little further down the line we can enjoy the convenience of throwing out the trunk (surprisingly, pre-aged stuff goes out of style at twice the speed of regular tat) *and* its contents at the same time.

Second-Baby Sex . . . Most newly wed Middlings can't wait to start breeding, for as soon as there is an organic bun in the oven we feel justified in going out and buying a much bigger car. However, once we have the baby (and the car) we feel a bit flat and know that to be a proper dysfunctional family we are going to need more children, which requires Second-Baby Sex. Second-Baby Sex isn't at all like honeymoon sex, affair sex or even rumpy pumpy. It is a means to an end and frankly a bit of a chore, involving timing graphs, baggy underpants, special diets and absolutely no Martinis or wacky baccy. This is why second children tend to be so much more rebellious: they haven't built up any resistance to vice in the womb (see our paper in *The Lance It* for more ~~nonsense~~ thorough investigative research).

Spots and Stripes . . . It is an irrefutable fact that Middle Class men will happily line up for Stripes on their socks, pants, shirts, suits, deckchairs, sporting costumes and butcher-style barbecue aprons, while Middle Class women go quite dotty for Spots on their pants, dresses, bikinis, teapots, aprons (stop us if this is getting sexist) frilly things, oven gloves, STOP!

Stock . . . Nothing tops off a household's Middling atmosphere better than the welcoming warming waft of three-day-old chicken Stock simmering on the AGA. In the old days, Stock came conveniently from cubes, which was very convenient, but now we have to make it ourselves from left-over organic chickens and any greenery we didn't know what to do with from our weekly veg box. Be sure to label your Stock properly before freezing it. We have spoiled many a hot summer's drinks party by defrosting what looked like elderflower cordial and serving it to the designated drivers, only to discover it was in fact chicken Stock.

Tweed . . . A sturdy Middle Class bottom, securely encased in Tweed skirt or trouserings, striding up a hill or down a dale is one of the finest sights the British countryside has to offer. As Oscar Fry once wittily ~~tweeded~~ tweeted while being measured for a pink tweed cravat, 'There is absolutely nothing twee about tweed.'

Thank-You Cards . . . If you ever feel uneasy that something just isn't quite right, you can be pretty sure as dammit that it will be to do with a Thank-you Card. Either you haven't sent one, and you know you really should, or you are owed a couple, which are more than a little overdue, not that you mind . . . but you do. Like singing 'Away in a Manger', it is something that children are far better at than grown-ups, and all the bribes, threats and actual violence are worth it when a ~~badly~~ charmingly spelled piece of folded A4 covered in scribbles and bits of pasta sauce comes through the letter box and thence ~~into the bin~~ on to the door of the fridge.

Ticking . . . Ticking ticks lots of Middling boxes: it's cheap, stripy and awfully versatile . . .

A Ticking Time Bomb

Tebay Services . . . Nothing says Middle Class bank holiday weekend more than sitting in a ~~yurt~~ traffic jam on the M6 heading to the Lake District. It is very tiresome, but a Middling tradition nonetheless. Once we get there we stay on the motorway, ignoring all the brown signs tempting us with stately homes, garden centres and tiggiwinkle-themed villages. There is only one hit destination in the Lake District these days: Tebay Services. There we load up on organic diesel, extra-virgin engine oil, locally sourced screen wash in the farm shop and drink ourselves into a stupor on unleaded wine in the 4-star restaurant.

Tutors . . . These are like tennis coaches, but for the brain and not as good looking. We pay them generously to come and teach Pelmet and Spartacus how to ~~roll long and complicated spliffs~~ pass exams during the gap between their disappointing GCSE results and their retakes. One hates to ask, of course, but one suspects that the Tutors are only available because they are also filling in time, between their disappointing university exam results and their retakes.

Tourists . . . Apart from our Budjet bumping into a mountain on the way to Italy, the only thing likely to ruin a Middle Class holiday is Tourists, or to give them their full title, *Bloody English Tourists.* These annoying people look and sound suspiciously like Middlings, what with their Panama hats, linen costumes and whatforth. They behave in a very inconsiderate manner, however, and keep cropping up in all the must-see places shouting at the natives when they don't understand them, clogging up the restaurants and asking if they take luncheon vouchers. Still, in some ways it is a nice thing to take our parents away on holiday with us.

Tattoos . . . Once the preserve of sailors and rogues, the Tattoo has enjoyed a remarkable leap in popularity amongst the Middle Classes in recent times, much to the horror of the parents . . .

Tea Towels . . . It has always been of the upmost importance that whenever you go to a National Trust house, national monument or Ford Open Prison that you buy a Tea Towel. They are usually the cheapest thing in the gift shop and make marvellous presents. All Middlings think 'you can never have too many Tea Towels', actually you can. Remember, never trust someone who only has chic and tasteful Tea Towels; like Dorian Gray, they will have a cupboard somewhere which towels the real story.

Trug Baskets . . . These mournful wood-lattice weavings are to be found in Middle Class houses and garden sheds, and have a sad story to tell. They were once used to transport dear little furry trugs from their burrows straight to the roasting oven, but the trugs were a victim of their own deliciousness and lack of sharp bitey teeth to defend themselves with, and were eaten to extinction by our Middling ancestors. In the 1960s the last trugs left in the wild recorded a song called 'Wild Thing' to highlight their plight. It was too little, too late. Now the only reminder that they ever existed is their baskets, which luckily are very useful for garden clippings.

Taxidermy . . . Victorian Middlings, with their love of nature, traversed the Empire shooting and stuffing every animal that moved. Quite soon there were none left, which annoyed their descendants so much that they threw all the Taxidermy out as soon as they inherited it. The only thing that generation *did* stuff was red peppers. Today, the moth-eaten-animal-in-a-glass-box look is back. This is because Algernon the Snow Leopard, preserved so wittily in plus fours playing golf, would have died by now anyway of natural causes; they don't need feeding; and no one is allergic to them, which makes it alright…doesn't it?

Thatch . . . No one in their right mind would ever want to own a thatched cottage, which is why the Daily Mail has taken control of the situation, bought them all up, called them not, 'money pits' or 'very flammable' but 'dream cottages' and intermittently gives them away as prizes to 'lucky' winners of competitions. They look absolutely charming of course when you're motoring past or seeing one on the local news surrounded by fire engines, but it costs as much to replace the roof every few years as it would to close the village school and send all the pupils to Eton.

Throws . . . Throws are the bits of material that these days we find ~~thrown~~ draped very carefully at the bottom of beds in hotels and other people's houses. In the old days a slightly bald, blancmange-pink Candlewick bedspread was the height of luxury. Now, thanks to the Internet and our Five-a-Day, we are evolving very quickly so we have *thrown* away the Candlewick and are decorating our beds with expensive offcuts from curtains, old ball gowns and witty patchworks made of tea towels we have retired from AGA-decoration duty. Throws are also very useful for hiding stains caused by the cat, dog or micro-pig, that have *thrown* up on the end of the bed.

Theatre . . . There is a certain type of Theatre production (i.e., all of them apart from musicals or pantos) which without Vintage Middlings would have no one in the seats to watch and be the audience. This is a shame because the Theatre ~~is always truly excellent~~ . . . ~~much more exciting than the cinema~~ . . . ~~culturally on the button~~ . . . makes for a lovely treat and you can buy little tubs of ice cream in the interval *and* have a couple of gins if you're quick about it.

Tennis . . . If you are thinking of embarking on a bout of doubles with some Middlings you've never played Tennis with before, it is important to ask them if they are any good. If they reply, 'Yes not bad' or, 'Pretty good actually', you'll be fine; they'll be as hopeless as you. If, however, they reply, 'Not really, my topspin is all over the shop at the mo and my backhand's unspeakable', quickly make your excuses and flee. If you remain you will be letting yourself in for an excruciating hour as the rest of the foursome pelt the ball at ferocious speeds around the court, very occasionally out of politeness sending it your way for you to bring the rally to a close by either missing it entirely, hitting it into the net or, worst of all, over the fence. On the plus side, you will have plenty of opportunities to say 'sorry'. This is why for most Middlings Tennis is a television programme watched in late June.

Thread Count . . . If you thought for a minute that as a good Middling you could relax having bought some nice Egyptian cotton bed linen, then think again. We have one word for you: Thread Count. OK that was two, but who's counting? Oh, that's right, WE ARE, Thread Counting, and if you take your Middle Class credentials seriously you are going to have to lie about your Thread Count (as well as telling your guests that the sheets haven't been slept in).

Thread Count Dracula

Trampolines . . . One of the best things about having neighbours is being able to ~~snoop over the fence~~ have chats over the fence about Cornucopia's maths grades since she became a Kumon black belt. Nowadays many Middlings have replaced their garden fences with wicker hurdles, which are just too high to allow us to snoop over effectively, and in these circumstances a Trampoline is vital as we can spy *and* exercise at the same time.

Tea . . . Middlings drink a lot of Tea, admittedly slightly less since we discovered real coffee and learned that Tea was packed with ant-accidents (being small, they get everywhere). The basic Middle Class Tea is of course Earl Grey. If you are after something a bit more punchy and what you actually want is a coffee but can't be bothered to wash up the cafetière, then you have what we call Builder's Tea. It is a misconception that this is what you should give your builders to drink. If you want the job finished on time, then only give them Slap Bang Poo Pong Platinum Snow Tips. They will knock through and re-plaster before you can say, 'But you quoted half that,' so they can get on to the next job and a decent cuppa . . .

Tap Water . . . There was a time when we would drink Tap Water at home and bottled water at restaurants, these days it is the other way round. We know that we are made of 80% water (the other 20% being either gin or elderflower cordial) and that Tap Water has passed through at least seven people. But because we are now all Middle Class that doesn't bother us anymore, and it would be very bad manners not to drink each other in public. Therefore, in restaurants, however tempting the sound of sparkling water is (to match our conversation), we tell the waiter sternly, 'No thank you, tap will be fine.' But weirdly at the end of the meal the jug is still full and we seem to have drunk forty bottles of house white.

Tree Houses . . . These used to be knocked up in an afternoon by Dad with nothing more than a ladder, some old planks, a hammer, nails and about four cans of McEwan's Export. These days they involve architects. The results speak for themselves. The modern Tree House does take a bit longer to construct, particularly if you're having a *Treehaüs* (three-storey Bauhaus style one that will need planning permission), and costs a bit more. But as Dad himself said when he'd finished ours just in time for England's second innings to start on the television, 'If a job's worth doing, it's worth doing well.'

Truffles . . . Thank goodness for all the cookery shows on television that have taught us the difference between the chocolate truffle and the savoury underground pig-hunted Truffle. It was a nightmare a few years ago when well-meaning foodie Middlings would serve you ravioli and then with solemn ceremony grate a large Thorntons rum truffle over it. The popularity of the savoury Truffle with Middlings has done wonders for the bank balances of many wily Italian peasants, who ~~pull them out of their sock drawers~~ hunt for them in a sustainable and local way, and explains all the ~~Ferrero Rochers~~ Ferraris outside almost every farmhouse in Tuscany, which had been puzzling us.

 **is for Unwelcome Non-Native Species...**

Uggs . . . If we Middlings know one thing, it is that the French are always right about fashion. This has led to some unfortunate confusion. Because no one has yet written a best-selling book called *Why French Women Don't Wear Uggs*, we assume that it is fine to wear them morning, noon and night. We know they may not look very stylish, but the important thing is that they are warm and comfy and all our friends wear them too. It is worth noting that there is no French translation for 'warm' *or* 'comfy'.

~~Ukaleyle~~ . . . ~~Ukolayle~~ . . . Ukulele . . . 'The unspellable played by the unmusical' *Oscar Fry*. But ignore grumpy old Oscar; these not only look like fun, they *are* fun. The bringing home of a Uke by a middle-aged Middle Class man is in no way a sign of an oncoming midlife crisis or a cry for help. Most people think they are small guitars. They are, in fact, incredibly small double bases, which makes a big small difference.

Unpasteurised Cheese . . . The problem with the act of pasteurisation is that it is French, and out of principle Middlings don't like the thought of a French Pastor fiddling about with our cheeses. Anyway, a mere French Pastor should have no authority in this country, being massively outranked by our native Stinking Bishop. Mind you, that's not saying much, the Stinking Bishop out*ranks* pretty much everything, certainly in our fridge.

Utility Rooms . . . This should really be an actual room, but there is no reason why the space under the kitchen work surface can't be referred to as a room (after all, trays often live there), particularly when you are in negotiations with the assistant at John Lewis. If you let slip that you don't have a designated Utility Room, John Lewis will not allow his appliances to come and live with you.

Union Jack . . . While the Americans are happy to wave their stars and stripes about in their ~~gardens~~ front yards, we Middlings find exuberant displays of patriotism rather vulgar outside Royal Jubilees or Royal Weddings. It's not that we don't feel a huge allegiance to our flag, it's just that being a discreet and understated people, we know the garden is not the place to show it . . .

oh no
there's even
a Union Jack Russell

Unwaxed Lemons . . . Since we discovered zest, Middlings have developed a keen interest in Unwaxed Lemons. This is a rather daring development, as an Unwaxed Lemon is a far cry from the glossy yellow citrus fruit we know and love. It is more Continental in appearance, sporting thick sprouts of hair growth in all manner of places. We recommend a compromise solution, the Brazilian Waxed Lemon.

unwaxed
lemon

waxed
lemon

Brazilian
Waxed
lemon

University . . . Once University was only for the Properly Posh, who went there to munch crumpets, talk about love and exercise pet lobsters. Later, it was for Middlings, who went there to *make* love, eat pasta, drink beer, put up posters and go on political marches. Now it is for everybody and we go there to catch sexually transmitted diseases and/or glandular fever, acquire massive overdrafts, watch daytime TV and eat pot noodles. As far as we know, at no stage in history has anyone ever gone there for the education. It is still essential for all Middlings to attend one, otherwise there'd be no reason to ever return from the gap year.

Using Foreign Words in English (and pronouncing them correctly) . . . We all pepper our conversation with foreign words, it's hard not to, but it is only Vintage Middlings who try to pronounce them correctly. Food is the prime area for this activity, and it is not uncommon for pasta dishes served in Middle Class kitchens to be sprinkled with *orrregganno*, *bazzzillicco* and *parrrmigianno* instead of marjoram, basil and parmesan cheese, which is very unpatriotic. And surely *chocolate pain* sounds like a much more intriguing accompaniment to a latte than a flakey old French *pain au chocolat*.

Underfloor Heating . . . It's been around since 500 BC, but most Middlings would prefer to think that it was invented about ten years ago. The reason being that if it was so jolly good, why did anyone bother to invent the radiator? Not a thought you want to have when you've just spent literally lots of money having the underfloor variety installed.

Volvos . . . Volvos were introduced to Britain by the Vikings, who brought them over by the longboat-load. Amazingly, some of these originals can still be seen at point-to-points, stately home car-boot sales or driving very slowly along country lanes.

Vanilla Pods . . . It turns out that these long, black, sticky beans are much more Middle Class than the little bottles of vanilla essence you can buy at the corner shop. They come in recyclable glass cigar tubes and, not surprisingly, are whoppingly expensive. The good news is that once you've scraped out the seeds to flavour your ~~scrambled eggs~~ custard, you can pop the used pod into a jar of sugar and make vanilla sugar! Of course, as the sugar jar often contains salt you will more than likely end up with vanilla salt, which would really surprise a visiting Scot about to tuck into his joyless morning porridge.

Visitors Books . . . These leather and vellum relics from the old days – before suitcases had wheels and an extending handle – are, rather like journals, a pain to fill in at the time but fascinating to look back on. Many a Middling is chilled by the words, 'Oh, you must write something in the visitors book before you go, there's some awfully funny stuff in there.' Suddenly any coherent thoughts and wit flee as you linger over your address before trying to offload the responsibility of the 'comments' box on to your spouse, child or au pair. By the time the spirit of Oscar Fry enters you and quite the funniest and most appropriate of sentiments pops into your brain, you're halfway home.

Vacherin . . . The world's whiffiest cheese comes in a round wooden box and is the ultimate Middling house present. Arriving for the weekend with one allows us to show off our foodie as well as our Middle Class credentials. Be very careful not to confuse it with La Vache qui Rit, which is also a cheese that comes in a round box. Inside this box are dear little wedges of cheese, flavoured with other cheese, and covered in silver paper, which is impossible to remove, gets stuck in our teeth and can cause toothache. If you are going to the Poshwolds for the weekend and take one of these in the hope of making a good impression, the 'rit' will be on you.

Views . . . Ever since E. M. Forrester followed his successful *Hornblower* series with the bonkbuster *Room with a View*, it has been very Middle Class to be aware of the importance of having Views. Both sorts.

Veg Boxes . . . The weekly arrival of a box of expensive unwashed organic veg on our doorsteps is one of the delights of being Middle Class. Once we've pressure-hosed all the mud off we become a contestant in our own *Ready Steady Cook*, as we try to work out what on earth we can conjure up with some celeriacs, turnips, carrots, an aubergine and some unidentifiable green leaves (they turned out to be sorrell). The one thing you can be sure of when you visit a Middling's house where they partake in a weekly Veg Box scheme, is the high quality, complexity and beauty of ~~the food they cook~~ their compost heaps.

Van Gogh . . . If there is one thing that Middlings agree on it is how wonderful the vibrant disturbed paintings of Mr Vincent Van Gogh are. The thing we can't agree on, however, is how to pronounce his name. Options include, phonetically: Van Goff, Van Go, Van Gog, Van Goo, Van Gosh and Van Guff. Far better to simply call him Vince and just because you don't agree with someone else's pronunciation, there is no need to chew their ear off about it.

Vinaigrette . . . Now that we eat bags and bags of bags of salad, Vinaigrette is playing a much more important role in our Middle Class lives. It used to be known as 'French dressing' and was always a bit sticky and stale. Now it is called *Vinaigrette* and if you casually offer your help in someone else's kitchen they will usually say, 'Oh, can you knock up a Vinaigrette for the salad?' This can be annoying because the ingredients for a Vinaigrette are normally scattered far and wide and you make quite a nuisance of yourself asking where everything is. It is, however, a very good opportunity to open all the dusty bottles of flavoured oil and vinegar, which we have in our cupboards but for some reason never open ourselves.

Vegetarianism . . . There are two types of Middling, those who eat meat and those who don't. Those who don't tend to be either teenage girls or very nice people. They need to be nice because they do get quite a lot of ~~steak~~ stick when they turn their nose up at our pigeon and squirrel pie and then groan when we offer them a mushroom risotto instead (apparently this is what they *always* get offered instead). Ironically it is the vegetarian Middlings who normally stay in Britain during the summer and have steakations. This is not because they love steak (they don't, obviously) it is because pretty much everywhere else in the world, apart from India, think vegetarians are mad and should be stoned to death, particularly the French.

Wooden Spoons . . . Middle Class kitchens are the perfect Wooden Spoon breeding ground. They need light, warmth and a large pot or jar to sit in near the AGA or range cooker. Once the first spoon has been installed, breeding will start of its own accord and carry on until, due to overcrowding, it will be almost impossible to remove one from the jar when you need it for beating the ~~children~~ roux. In Scottish households there is sometimes cross-pollination between spoons and spurtles, which can make tasting the soup quite challenging.

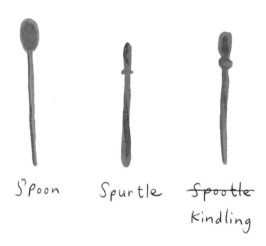

S'poon   Spurtle   ~~Spootle~~ Kindling

The Week (magazine) . . . It is very important for Middlings to know what's going on in the world, and even though the news is available on tap 24 days a week, annoyingly we don't have time to keep up with it due to Pilates, sorting through the veg box and foraging. *The Week* was invented for people just like us, so on Fridays we can go to stay with friends for the weekend and have lots of opinions on everything — which amazingly are the same as everyone else's.

The Wagon . . . Something Middlings regularly climb on to and then normally fall off again very quickly.

Wind Chimes . . . These have only recently become Middle Class and acceptable as additions to gardens and gazebos. Now that we have discovered their charming oriental tinklings and chimings, we find them indispensable, particularly in the Poshwolds, where they are fabulous for drowning out the constant and frankly rather irritating whirring of wind turbines, and the hummings from solar panels we have ecologically installed on the roof ~~to make tax free money out of the national grid~~ to do our bit for the planet.

Wild Swimming . . . This was bound to happen. What with most Middle Class swimming pools being so cluttered up with inflatable cartoon characters, floating furniture, lilos and children, swimming in them is almost impossible. Once we would just have taken our clothes off on the riverbank, gone in for a dip and thought no more about it. But that isn't progressive enough for Middlings, who like to put on wetsuits and turn things into proper activities, so now we have Wild Swimming. Picnics are also about to be rebranded *wild* eating and reading a book under a tree, *wild* reading. We yearn for something a bit more challenging, like *wild* golf.

Wills . . . These used to be things that our parents drew up to make sure we got all the money they had ~~spent their lives working hard for~~ inherited from their parents. Thanks to heart replacements, lung replacements, hip replacements and, in extreme cases heart, lung *and* hip replacements, our Vintages ~~go on and on~~ have got much better life expectancy. This means they have time to spend all *our* inheritance on cruises and *Daily Telegraph* offers for vital must'aves like walk-in roll-top baths and Viagra. So we're not really sure if now — despite the Alessi garlic crushers, cheap flights to Montenegro and Emma Bridgewater bunting — *is* actually the best time in history to be Middle Class after all.

Wild Garlic . . . The problem with being Middle Class and shopping from the hedgerow is that the only thing we can sniff out with absolute confidence is Wild Garlic. This leads to overkill in garlic season, as first-time foragers, keen to get in on the act, can rather overuse it. Heston Verytall might be able to get away with turning flavour conventions on their heads, but when our friends serve us panna cotta for pudding scattered with Wild Garlic flowers, we can't wait for spring to be over (the flowers are, of course, *much* better in a sorbet).

Waitrose . . . With its wide aisles, generous lighting, ethical sourcing policy and the fact that it's always full of our friends, Waitrose is Middle Class for supermarket. What Waitrose stands for, *we* stand for; if they say eat it, *we* eat it; what they consider essential, *we* consider essential. (Imagine a world where blueberries, hummus and truffle oil aren't considered essential — it is not a world *we* would like to live in!) Waitrose? We're not waiting, let's go shopping! (And *yes,* we will have another bag for life, you *can't* have too many!)

Winter Sun . . . Our ancestor Middlings used to show off their Middle Class credentials by staying inside all year nibbling arsenic and chalk to make sure their complexions exactly matched Farrow & Ball's Corpse White. These days we aspire to a very different colour scheme, especially in winter. There is nothing that says 'we're doing rather well, thank you' better than popping up in mid February with a face the colour of an antique Welsh ~~crooner~~ dresser. The fun doesn't stop there as our friends turning Envy Green sets us off to an even better advantage.

Wellingtons . . . It is really exasperating that for so long Wellington Boots (named after one of the Wombles) were only available in green or black. It is hard to imagine things like the Irish Potato Famine or the Clearance of the Glens getting everyone so depressed, had the peasants been wearing Wellies decorated with funky spots or pretty bows. Wellies (as they are more commonly known), which were once the most Middle Class of things, have of late been elevated to the status of 'worldwide fashion phenomenon', and there are even rumours that ~~actress~~ . . . ~~model~~ . . .Poshwold pig farmer Liz Wurzley is developing a line of super lightweight slingback party wellies ~~which is exciting~~.

Mummy, they *are* following me... I don't like it!

Wisteria . . . Apart from draping it in Union Jack bunting, having a Wisteria on the front of our houses is the best way of informing passing burglars that this is a Middle Class home and probably stuffed with silver. The burglars are particularly grateful that the Wisteria is our plant of choice, as it means they don't have to drive around with ladders pretending they are window cleaners, and can just shin up its sturdy trunk and climb through the bedroom windows we like to leave open on account of our fondness for fresh air. Apart from this slight drawback, Wisteria is actually very useful for hiding the pebble dash we couldn't afford to remove due to the surprisingly high final cost of the knocking through.

WI . . . Now that most Middle Class women already have black belts in knitting, baking and jam boiling, they yearn to return to more innocent times and are joining the WI in droves to learn the ancient traditional crafts of belly dancing, pole dancing and striptease.

Wetsuits . . . Where once British beaches were awash with toddlers and children turning a pleasing pink, they are now dotted with little bodies clad in black neoprene with stripes of DayGlo green and pink. We think this might be because the parsimonious parents totted up the figures and worked out that it was cheaper and less effort to squeeze Perseus and Loggia into Wetsuits than to constantly apply suncream. It also makes it easier to keep an eye on them abroad, as children from other nations do not seem to be so sensitive to water temperature, possibly because exposure to cold water has improved their circulations.

Weddings . . . Weddings are an opportunity for Middle Class women to show off their self-restraint. There is a big fat gypsy Wedding inside every Middling mother and daughter that's struggling to get out, and unfortunately normally does. No sooner have the Banns been read than the bunting is gilded, the Wedding Planner has ordered a cake (a life-size replica of the bride's first pony) and the local B&Bs are redecorated to match the bridesmaids' dresses. But no matter how much money we throw at the thing, it is reassuring to know that by the time the bride and groom have left in his 'n' hers matching helicopters, the same multi-generational mishmash of embarrassing dancing and drunken groping will be unfolding on the dance floor and, at really good ones, bare-knuckle boxing in the car park.

Wood-Burning Stoves . . . Woodburners are now quite as Middle Class as AGAs, much cheaper to run, and, if you don't mind the smell of burnt sausage on your silk curtains, more useful for cooking on. However, rather like other people's dishwashers, compost bins and wives, they should be approached with care. Having finally mastered the art of operating your own Eazi-Lite, double-gusset, buttress-sliding, vented, clear flue stove does not guarantee success with anyone else's. This is particularly true of those found in glamping yurts. In order to avoid hypothermia on the first night of our summer holiday, we always take a gallon of paraffin, an entire Sunday newspaper and some pine cones, which usually does the trick.

Wine . . . Wine is a Middle Class currency. We pay for going to dinner with friends and accept it (often the very same bottle) from them in return. Some ~~cold hearted~~ financially astute Middlings buy it as a ~~drinkable~~ sensible investment. And some rich Middlings are lucky enough to inherit cellars full of it (until Varsity and Exactamundo's eighteenth birthday parties, when it all vanished). One thing is sure, at some stage of your life you will find yourself signed up to a Wine Club. Like the friend you make during your first week at uni who you can never shake off, no matter how often you change your address, your name, and even your sex, you will be pursued by cases of fruity Zinfandel from 'South America's most exciting new wine-growing region' for the rest of your life.

Working From Home . . . As we have all made our homes so incredibly nice, it is hardly surprising that we can't bear to leave them and go to work. For those brave enough to take the leap and 'Work' From Home, there are some rules. It is fine to spend an extra hour in bed, because that hour would otherwise be spent commuting. You *don't* have to get out of your dressing gown all day; that would be a waste of time. And it is essential, before you start work, to do all the little jobs that, not being done, make working impossible, like pumping up the tyre on the wheelbarrow and cleaning the inside of the fridge. Few people who go to an office have any idea how busy you actually are all day . . . signing for other people's parcels and looking after them until they get back from work.

This is ridiculous, I can't possibly get any work done until I've descaled the kettle

← Other People's parcels

X-ray . . . It is hard to think of anything much more Middle Class than an X-ray. What is the first thing we think of when Xander falls out of the tree house and snaps his arm? X-ray. What does the vet suggest when the Labrador swallows the Alessi garlic crusher? X-ray. Really *ever* so Middle Class indeed.

Xylophone . . . Another of those things that literally screams Middle Class and is not just in this book because there aren't any genuine Xs out there. What Middling home doesn't boast a Xylophone in either the toy cupboard or the music room, I ask you? To hear little Xanthe plonking her way through ~~The Arrival of the Queen~~ of ~~Sheba~~ 'Twinkle, Twinkle Little Star' on the Xylophone is one of Middle Class life's greatest pleasures.

XOX (kisses) . . . In a deliberate thrust to appear more liberated than our stiff Victorian forebears, Middlings have taken up greeting one another with kisses. Rather like deciding as a nation to start driving on the other side of the road, this has led to plenty of accidents. The Continentals make it look easy, but *we* never seem to know which cheek to go for, or more importantly, how many kisses to attempt. It is no surprise that some people use the confusion as an excuse to go straight for the lips, when the alternative is a mouthful of hair, an ear, or just thin air. We also like to show how friendly we are by signing off our emails, text messages and letters with Xs to represent our kisses. There are many subtle nuances depending on the amount, spacing and case of these kisses, but we think the basics are that: x is a friendly peck, X is a French kiss, O is a hug and OXO is a brand of gravy granules.

XL or XS . . . Many Middlings struggle to buy clothes the right size, particularly on the Internet, where there aren't any changing rooms. Generally, small people buy clothes that are too small for them and big people buy clothes that are too big for them. This is a strange psychological phenomenon, which isn't helped by the fact that the people at the sizing department keep suffering finger fits when touching the X button, so you now see size options that go from XXXXS – which must be for baby dwarves – to XXXXL – which are for Americans.

X (10 in Roman Numerals) . . . There is something sublimely Middle Class about Roman Numerals. To be able to understand them beyond number III (three) shows instantly that you are an educated person to be reckoned with. The opportunity to show off your ability to read them is somewhat limited, unless you watch a lot of BBC television, where they flash up the date the programme was made in Roman Numerals at the end of the credits. It is not a brilliant return on the time spent mastering them to be able to say at the end of a repeat of *The Goodies*, 'Hmm, made in 1976; hasn't aged that well . . .' because by then, everyone else would have already left the room or stabbed themselves to death.

Xenophobia . . . This is a condition Middlings are proud not to suffer from. On the whole, we think that Xenos (foreigners) are rather fun, what with their funny costumes and strange way of speaking English. If at first a Xeno doesn't understand you, then keep repeating your question or command, getting progressively louder until they do.

BeatriX Potter . . . In all the canon of English literature it is hard to think of a more Middle Class cannonball than Beatrix Potter. Grandmother of Harry Potter, she never fully recovered from his parents' death at the hands of the furry and seemingly charming Vole de Morte. Shortly afterwards, to help deal with the trauma, she wrote her cathartic masterpiece *Jemima Puddleduck*. Beatrix was beset by bad luck, and when her fiancée lost his carrot crop to rabbits, she vowed she would be avenged and devoted the rest of her life to torturing small furry animals by writing about them.

Lord Vole de Mort

Xpats . . . Apart from the criminals on the Costa del Coffee, it is probably fair to say that most Ex-pats are Middle Class. The first year of Expattery is always the most enjoyable; you spend it discovering markets, finding restaurants and marvelling at the price of booze. All your friends are jealous and wish they were as brave as you. After that it's downhill, and you end up very bored and completely alcoholic. You can't come home and be a Pat again, because that would be an admission of defeat, and besides, you can't afford to pay £20 for your now daily bottle of gin.

Xhibitions . . . Without Middlings, Exhibitions wouldn't exist. There are two main types of Exhibition: those in enormous galleries, where you pay to get in but can't buy the art; and those in small private galleries, which are free to get in but you can buy the art. The former type can be a bit of a bore. There is a sort of unspoken expectation for you to attend must-see Exhibitions, a summons honoured by countless other Middlings, and you're lucky to escape with nothing worse than an overpriced catalogue and a cold. The latter variety are more fun and include as much free wine as you need to realise that what at first looked totally ~~crap~~ derivative is in fact rather fun and quite a bargain for sheven hundred pounds.

X-husbands and Wives . . . Like everyone else, Middlings do sometimes tire of their spouses, which is hardly surprising when you consider how long we live and that marriage was invented in the days when you were lucky to last past forty. But Middlings will insist on trying to be friends with their exes, for the sake of Arabica and Maximus, when we would, if we're honest, far rather hear that they'd been eaten feet first by the lions at Longleat.

 **is for Yummy Mummies**

(the ancient curse of)...

Yoga . . . 'A quiet sports hall full of flexible women in leotards, the silence only broken by the occasional fart', as Oscar Fry once remarked (wittily of course). Middlings are attracted to Yoga by the 'keep fit', spiritual and ethnic aspects. There is also something vaguely rock and roll about it, didn't the Beatles do Yoga? (Or are we thinking of Bananarama?) Anyway, after the success of Toga Parties in the 1970s, some dyslexics started throwing Yoga Parties by mistake, which inevitably led to the two being combined – YogaToga parties. These were *very* rude, and we think it's pretty likely that we were conceived at one.

Yeast Extract . . . Better known by it's other name – Marmite. This has long been a favourite Middle Class salty spread, with its tasteful old-fashioned packaging and the fact that you get your money's worth as it lasts for ages. The Properly Posh and *some* Middlings have solid silver lids for theirs, which are very smart. You can tell if you're in a Properly Posh household as they throw theirs away with the jar when it's finished. No Middling would ever do this

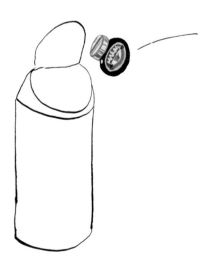

Yorkshire . . . Not exactly awash with Middlings, and those that are there aren't easy to spot, what with the fog and their moorland-coloured costumes. If you get close up you *can* identify them by their corduroys, dogs (Labradors, Spaniels or Jack Russells), their Land Rovers and their involvement in small-scale cheese production. If you hear what you *think* is a Middling on a foggy dale, endlessly screaming 'CATHY!', then move on; he *isn't* Middle Class, the swine.

Yacht clubs . . . A lacht of racht is written about Yacht Clubs, the truth of the matter is that they have standards that they enjoy maintaining. It is reassuring to know that there are some portals even a Middling cannot enter without a jacket, tie, trousers with a crease down the middle, sou'wester, pipe, beard and yellow wellies. The real success of them lies in the fact that unlike actual ~~yots~~ yachts, they are nice and stable. Were you to ask anyone standing on the veranda of one, ~~rum~~ pink gin in hand, whether they actually owned a yacht, they would reply to a man that they didn't, they loved the clothes and the scene but unfortunately were afflicted by terrible seasickness so the club was the next best thing. (No idea if this is true, we tried to get into a Yacht Club to conduct the poll, but our trouser creases had become smoothed out on the bus ride there and entry was barred.)

Yoghurt . . . One of the greatest improvements in Middle Class life over the past thirty years has been the proliferation in flavours of Yoghurt. Although, since the fruit corner the innovations have slowed down a little. If you are very Middle Class, there is a good chance that you may have made your own yoghurt, in the airing cupboard. We certainly did, but one drunken night when we had a few people stay over after the ~~pub~~ opera, one of them mistook the warm off-white mixture for a duvet cover and poured it all over the sofa bed. He didn't smell very nice the next morning but at least his girlfriend's thrush had cleared up.

Yurts . . . Very short for yoghurt and actually completely different. These domed and portable homes were designed in the harsh landscapes of the Northern Steppes by Mongolian nomads for the use of British Middlings as a rather fun spare room in their gardens in Dorset or for glamping weekends in the Poshwolds.

'You must know . . .' When a Middling meets someone new we are in a state of terrible unease until we have discovered what people we know in common. It doesn't normally take long to unearth one or two mutual friends or friends of friends, and amongst more gregarious Middlings this will keep them busy all night. If you're struggling, then the temptation is to give in and lie, saying, 'Yes, I think I *do* know Freddie Cumsocks! Met him at uni/Cornwall/wine-tasting holiday in Puglia.' DON'T DO THIS ANYMORE. What with cleverphones and so forth, your new acquaintance will, with genuine delight and excitement, Tweet him and you will be exposed in a trice as a Fraudling.

is for ~~Zoos~~ Conservation Centres...

Zoom Lollies . . . Zoom Lollies and their stable mates the Fab, which still exist after all these years, have recently been rediscovered by the Middle Class. They didn't used be Middle Class, as they were stuffed with E-numbers and were among the cheap options at the bottom of the chest freezer in the corner shop. Middlings have always preferred choc ices, Cornettos or, if you were a bit short, a Mini Milk. Developed by NASA, the Zoom Lolly is an exact replica of an actual rocket. When they first came out, during the Cold War, they were very hard to get your hands on as Soviet scientists kept buying them to study the design. To this day, the aerodynamic shape means you can get a Zoom in your mouth much faster than a Flake 99.

Zinc . . . Most Middlings enjoy their Zinc galvanised, onto buckets, chicken wire and so forth – but some very ~~rich~~ sophisticated ones use it neat on their kitchen worktops. It is rather lovely because, like pewter, it has a pewtery look about it. For people who are very jealous of those that have Zinc worktops there are Zinc pills available. They don't make the jealousy go away entirely, but they do help with many of the symptoms, like the green eyes.

I am NOT jealous of my sister! It's just she's literally got EVERYTHING, even the kitchen's zinc!

Zoopla . . . Nosey Middlings spend hours on this property website ~~spying~~ innocently enquiring as to the value of everyone's houses. The assumption is always that Zoopla has overestimated other people's while massively underestimating ours. The reason for this is that no one from Zoopla has ever actually been to our house to see for themselves our stunning use of French Grey Eggshell and the knocking through we've just carried out in an upstairs cupboard, which must have added a few thou' to the value.

Zumba . . . The worldwide success of this fitness regime is not down entirely to the British Middle Classes, but we have certainly helped. It is a combination of all the world's sexiest dances, excluding Morris. In fact, it is an opportunity for a roomful of women to thrust wildly to music and wiggle their bottoms and get incredibly sweaty while eyeballing a well ~~endowed~~ toned Latino man and not get pregnant. It is hard to see the appeal.

Zest . . . Middlings have always used Zest, but with restraint, scraping a few atoms of the stuff into cakes and biscuits. However, since the discovery of Italian cooking and microplane graters, we are now tipping great piles of it (along with finger flesh) into all manner of things. Were this a cookery book, we would expound on the transforming powers the addition of a melange of finely zested lemon, raw garlic and parsley gives stews and soups once they're cooked, but it isn't, so we won't . . .whoops! (Maybe we should do a cookery book? As everyone knows, writing a cookbook is easy peasy lemon ~~squeezy~~ zesty . . .)

Ziplok Bags . . . These rolls of little plastic bags are very much the Middling's friend. They are just the thing for dealing with leftovers and gluts, as, once filled, they can be conveniently popped into the fridge, freezer or bin. The problem with Ziplok Bags is that they feel so substantial, with their little blue sliding zip, that unlike the Americans who invented them, we are loathe to throw them away and we try and wash them out and re-use them. The washing bit is hard enough, what with all the turning inside out; but drying is well-nigh impossible. Dog owners have found another use for Ziplok Bags, after which they rarely get reused.

Zipcars . . . Middlings, being environmentally minded, have taken to Zipcars with gusto. For those not in the know, a Zipcar is a special kind of rental car made entirely out of recycled zips. They are quite easy to operate, but the total absence of buttons inside takes a bit of getting used to.

Zzzz . . . It is perfectly Middle Class to fall asleep when you've just finished reading or writing quite a long book. But remember, in the words of ~~Oscar Fry~~ Anthony Burgess, 'Laugh and the world laughs with you, snore and you sleep alone' . . .

With thanks to:

Ed Barber

Jo Crocker

Sophie de Brant

Sue Denim

Eugenie Furniss

Catherine Gibbs

Jo Gledhill

Fi Glover

Chris Gossage

Charlotte Greig

Antonia Hanbury

David Hayles

Christian Hodell

Rebecca Nicolson

Roland Philipps

From Byron, Austen and Darwin

to some of the most acclaimed and original
contemporary writing, John Murray takes pride in
bringing you powerful, prizewinning, absorbing
and provocative books that will entertain you
today and become the classics of tomorrow.

We put a lot of time and passion into what we
publish and how we publish it, and we'd like to
hear what you think.

Be part of John Murray – share your views with us at:

www.johnmurray.co.uk

 johnmurraybooks

 @johnmurrays

 johnmurraybooks

Local Colour

Good Ordinary
Claret

Spaniel

Wild Garlic
Pesto

Frost-Proof
Terracotta

Poshwold Dreams

Roof-Box
Grey

Rare Breed
Cowpat

Ambridge
Green

Uncooked
Lobster